Contents

Alcoholism and Pathological Gambling

Similarities and Differences

Arthur G. Herscovitch

Learning Publications, Inc.
Holmes Beach, Florida

ISBN 1-55691-146-7

Learning Publications, Inc.
5351 Gulf Drive
P.O. Box 1338
Holmes Beach, FL 34218-1338

Printing: 5 4 3 2 1   Year: 3 2 1 0 9

Printed in the United States of America

About the Author

Dr. Herscovitch is a clinical psychologist who has been on staff with the Addictions Foundation of Manitoba in Winnipeg, Manitoba, Canada for 22 years. Besides being on staff with the A.F.M., he also has a private practice and is an assistant professor of psychology with the School of Medicine at the University of Manitoba.

Dr. Herscovitch is a member of the Canadian Psychological Association, the Manitoba Psychological Society, and is certified to practice psychology by the Psychological Association of Manitoba and the Canadian Register of Health Services Providers in Psychology. He also sits on the Advisory Board to the Addictions Intervention Association in Canada. He has lectured on the topics of alcoholism, chemical dependence, and pathological gambling, both in Canada and in the United States.

Dr. Herscovitch's publications include these books: *Alcoholism: From Recognition to Recovery, Drug Dependence: From Recognition to Recovery, Cocaine: The Drug and the Addiction,* and *Everything You Need to Know About Drug Abuse.*

Preface

This book should help treatment professionals recognize when a gambling disorder exists, and further, it should function as an aid in terms of the application of treatment strategies to those who suffer from pathological gambling.

This book compares alcoholism and pathological gambling, demonstrating both the differences and the overwhelming similarities between the two disorders. Included is information about why some individuals are both substance abusers and pathological gamblers and some are addicted to one but not both drugs and gambling. These addictive disorders, the diagnostic information, and the psychological, physical, and social processes that sustain the disorders and progression are discussed. Where relevant, case studies are used to clarify concepts. Recovery and treatment information is also provided.

This book is written for professionals (psychologists, physicians, social workers, teachers, counselors, probation officers, lawyers, etc.) and lay individuals.

1
Historical Perspective

Both alcohol consumption and gambling are long-established phenomena. It appears that alcohol consumption has been around since prehistoric times. The use of fermented beverages has been established since the late stone age (Core Knowledge 1978) and beer, fermented from barley, may indeed be the oldest alcohol drink. Alcohol consumption was an integral part of many ancient cultures including those of the Egyptians, Greeks, and Romans. Alcohol was consumed as part of cultural and religious ceremonies, and a variety of wines were produced for such purposes. In areas of the world where grapes could not be grown, alcohol beverages were made from other products such as barley, wheat, and related crops. In Europe during the Middle Ages, physicians and pharmacists believed that alcohol had medicinal value. Depending upon the culture, alcohol was valued as a remedy for a great variety of human maladies, including ailments of the intestines, liver, and spleen. Distilled liquors were widely used in Europe at this time, because of their purported healing value, which in turn encouraged social consumption. The early colonists of North America brought with them their cultural habits of alcohol consumption, and, as a consequence, the drinking of alcohol was an implicit part of the developing North-American culture.

Until the eighteenth century, there was minimal public awareness of or concern for the harmful consequences of excessive drinking. For example, during the 1700's in Britain, wide-spread alcohol consumption was condoned, because of the revenue it provided for the Government. It was not until gin drinking, in particular, became so rampant in England that prohibition became a major political issue. However, despite periods of public concern, alcohol consumption has, over the ages, remained a significant part of most cultures and has effectively survived negative sanctions and even prohibitionary periods in some countries.

Since the late 1950's and early 1960's, the traditional patterns of intoxicant use have literally exploded to include many different types of drugs, including the abuse of some that are medically prescribed. In spite of the competition from a plethora of both licit and illicit mood-altering substances and the increased public concern over the harmful effects of over-indulgence, alcohol consumption still remains popular.

It is only in the last fifty years that we have come to understand that alcoholism is a disease, not a product of immorality or weak will. And, it is only in the last forty or so years that centers have been developed for treatment of alcoholism.

It appears that public concern about gambling became manifest long before the concern about alcohol consumption. Some people were recognized as gambling addicts long before addiction was associated with heavy drinking (Rosenthal 1992). For example, during ancient Roman times, gambling was rampant, and gamblers who could not pay their debts, were sometimes sentenced into slavery by the courts. According to Rosenthal (1992), pathological (compulsive) gambling was the first addiction to be publicly recognized.

The natives indigenous to North America had their own forms of gambling. When North America was settled by the Europeans, the early settlers brought with them their types of gambling, including card and dice games. As of 1980, legalized gambling in one form or another has been allowed in most of the United States, and gambling is rapidly gaining popularity in Canada.

Currently, a majority of adults in Canada and the United States consume alcohol either occasionally or regularly, and a significant number participate in gambling activities, either occasionally or regularly. However, of the people who consume alcohol and/or gamble, only a small proportion develop problems. A study conducted in the United States, between 1980 and 1985, indicates that about 8 percent of the adult population showed some symptoms of alcohol dependence (American Psychiatric Association D.S.M. IV 1994). With reference to pathological gambling, studies estimate the incidence to be between 1.2 percent to about 3.4 percent of the adult population (Volberg 1990; Volberg and Steadman 1988; Volberg and Steadman 1989; Culleton 1985).

In Canada and the United States, gambling revenues are rapidly becoming a major source of income for both provincial and state governments. However, as more people gamble, more develop problems with gambling. In response, treatment programs are becoming increasingly available.

When the behaviors of gambling and alcohol consumption are analyzed, commonalities are evident. For example, people gamble and consume alcohol for similar reasons. As well, not all individuals who gamble or consume alcohol develop problems. However, of those who do, similarities are also evident. Chapter 2 compares the similarities and the differences in why people first start drinking and gambling, and why many persist.

2

Why Do People Gamble and Consume Alcohol ?

Over the centuries, both gambling and alcohol consumption have endured as popular activities. They are so popular, that even when it is illegal, many people will gamble or drink. People start to gamble, or consume alcohol, for similar reasons. The reasons for maintaining both activities are also similar.

Curiosity

People are implicitly curious. They like to try and experience new things. Many people begin gambling out of curiosity. They read about gambling, hear people talking about it, or see gambling on television or in the movies. If an individual tries one game of chance and happens to enjoy it, the pleasure can fuel his or her curiosity to sample other forms of gambling. Winning at gambling, even small amounts, often adds incentive to continue gambling.

Like gambling, curiosity is a factor in why some people sample alcohol. They see people drinking, hear people talking about it, and see it romanticized. Again, like gambling, if a person consumes alcohol and enjoys either the effects or the taste, he or she may often seek other opportunities to drink. As well, sampling one type of alcohol often sparks a person's interest in other types.

However, unlike alcohol, many people engage in some form of gambling at a fairly young age; often considerably younger than what they are when they start drinking. Children commonly use the term "bet," with a clear understanding of what it means or even make simple bets. Their reasons for betting are often based upon their trying to outdo friends. For example, a child may bet a friend that he can run faster, and he may even wager a prized possession. By the time children reach their early teens, they've usually had more extensive experience with gambling, than with drinking.

Once a person has engaged in one form of a particular activity, that individual's inhibitions against engaging in further related activities, are usually weakened (Bandura 1969). In other words, once a person has tried gambling or drinking, his or her inhibitions against gambling or drinking again, or trying different forms of gambling, or types of alcohol, are weakened.

Enjoyment

If an activity is pleasurable, the pleasure becomes a major incentive for engaging in the activity. Regardless of whether they win or lose, the act of gambling is pleasurable to many. Gambling has been referred to as an ego-syntonic activity (Rosenthal 1992), in that it is both enjoyable and exciting. Some individuals discover, however, that gambling produces more than mere enjoyment — it results in euphoria. In other words, gambling has greater significance for some people, than for others. For many, even the thought of gambling provides a sense of pleasure. There are also people who feel deprived when they stop gambling or if they are prevented from doing so.

The same processes apply to alcohol consumption. For many people, consuming alcohol is an enjoyable act. They relish the taste of their beverage and the effects it has on them. As with gambling, drinking is more important for some people than for others. As well, there are those who feel let down when they are prevented from drinking.

Escape

While some people first start gambling for the anticipated enjoyment, some rapidly discover that gambling is an effective means of escape. They find that gambling relieves them of depression, boredom, loneliness, and other types of discomfort. Some individuals start gambling and become "disconnected" from their emotions. When gambling, they enter a reverie, completely distracted from uncomfortable thoughts and feelings.

For some individuals, alcohol consumption functions similarly, in that drinking provides them with a sense of escape. They rapidly learn that drinking provides relief from their woes. After a few drinks, uncomfortable feelings dissipate and unpleasant thoughts are dulled. Because of their effectiveness as vehicles for relief, both alcohol consumption and gambling are popular.

Immediate Gratification

Whether people gamble or consume alcohol for enjoyment or as a means of escape, the effects are immediate.

When gambling or drinking, people discover that enjoyment comes quickly, and discomfort is rapidly eliminated. Even the thought or anticipation of gambling or drinking, provides a sense of relief for some people. The immediate gratification enhances the popularity of both gambling and drinking.

However, gambling or drinking for immediate gratification, is not without its drawbacks. In their never-ending quest for instant satisfaction, some people find themselves gambling more frequently and for longer periods. However, to achieve their desired level of pleasure or relief, they increase the size of their bets. For a time, small bets were adequate, but then larger bets become a must. A parallel process occurs with alcohol consumption. To reach their level of pleasure or relief, some individuals find themselves drinking more frequently and for longer periods to achieve their gratification. As well, larger quantities of alcohol are now required to produce the same effect of lesser quantities in the beginning.

While the process of immediate gratification appears to work the same for both gambling and alcohol consumption, the specific nature of the process varies. With gambling, some individuals report a euphoria akin to "living on the edge." They become highly stimulated by not knowing whether they will win or lose. To intensify the euphoria, some gamblers increase the size of their bets. Typically, drinking alcohol frequently results in the opposite feeling. Although some people may engage in exciting activities while consuming alcohol, the effect of the alcohol is sedation.

Peer Pressure

Peer pressure is a powerful force that often plays a significant role in one's drinking and gambling behavior. The need to be liked and accepted by others is a very powerful motivator of human behavior (Freedman 1978). Susceptibility to peer pressure usually develops in childhood. Because almost all of a young child's needs are satisfied by others, children rapidly come to associate gratification of their needs with acceptance by others. This gratification first occurs through their parents. Later the gratification comes from friends, teachers, relatives, and other significant people. As children mature, they tend to be more selective in choosing friends, gravitating toward those who can satisfy their needs and provide acceptance. Children learn to alter their behavior to meet the needs of their friends.

Besides wanting to be liked and accepted by others, individuals have a fear of being deviant (Freedman 1978). Children quickly learn that behavior that is too different from the norm often leads to ridicule and rejection. The process of wanting acceptance from others, combined with a fear of being deviant, is the basis of peer pressure. In essence, peer pressure is the influence from one's group to act in a manner consistent with the norms of the group. Sensitivity to peer pressure is developed in childhood and stays with the individual throughout adulthood. Peer pressure functions in the same manner at every age. Whether a group of children is influencing a child to play tag, a teen-age group is pressuring another teen to skip classes, or professionals press for all to adopt a dress code, peer pressure is present.

In the case of gambling and alcohol consumption, peer pressure is frequently influential in both the development and the maintenance of both behaviors. If one's friends drink or gamble, there is often pressure to follow suit. One risks alienation by resisting the peer pressure. This is especially the case if social events involve gambling or drinking.

Modeling and Imitation

We learn new behaviors by observing the behavior of others and noticing the consequences. If the results of a particular action are desirable, an observer will most likely act similarly. For example, if an individual observes another enjoying a particular food, this increases the chance of the observer also eating the food. However, if a person observes another experiencing undesirable results, the observer will probably act differently.

Several factors, most of which are attributable to the model (the individual being imitated), are predictive of imitative behavior. The behaviors of people who are perceived to be socially competent, of higher socio-economic status, and of high intelligence, are more likely to be imitated than the behaviors of those who are perceived to lack these attributes (Bandura 1969).

With reference to gambling behavior, modeling influences are significant. Children, in particular, are very susceptible to modeling influences, especially those of their parents. Because children perceive their parents as being competent, they frequently emulate the behavior of their parents. This includes television-watching habits, eating patterns, involvement in sports, and so on. The same applies to gambling. If a child observes his or her parents gambling and obviously enjoying the activity, the child comes to associate gambling with having fun. This, of course, increases the chances of that child becoming a gambler. The National Information Center on Legalized and Compulsive Gambling (1991) found that the majority of teen-agers who gamble, were exposed to that activity by their parents and/or relatives. Not only is the behavior of gambling imitated by children, but also patterns of gambling. For example, Ladouceur and Mireault (1988) found that high school students who had gambling problems were more likely to have parents who had problems with gambling than were students who did not have a problem with gambling. Also, children usually adopt a form of gambling that is the same as their parents (Bergh and Kuhlhorn 1994).

Not only do models teach people new behaviors, but they are also influential in weakening inhibitions in observers. If an individual is uncertain about engaging in an activity, but observes someone else enjoying that activity, the observation weakens the individual's inhibitions. An individual's inhibitions against gambling, for example, may be weakened by observing a friend, parent, or relative engaging in the activity and enjoying it. Even watching strangers gamble, weakens a person's inhibitions.

The same modeling processes apply to alcohol consumption. Children, for example, observe their parents and others drinking and having fun, which usually prompts a desire in them to do the same. Watching virtually anyone consume alcohol and enjoy it can weaken inhibitions against drinking. Braucht (1982) summarizes evidence indicating a greater chance of problem drinking among adolescents who come from families of heavy drinkers in which there is minimal parental disapproval of their drinking. He also states, that adolescent problem drinkers tend to belong to peer groups in which heavy drinking is modeled, and peer approval for alcohol consumption exists. In this case, there is a combination of peer pressure and modeling influences. Further, Braucht states that adolescents who are heavy drinkers have parents who are less involved with them. In other words, not only do these parents model patterns of excessive alcohol consumption, but they also fail to model healthy interactive behaviors.

Typically, the children of parents who rely almost exclusively upon gambling or drinking as a means of recreation or stress reduction are not exposed to healthy behaviors. Lacking healthy behaviors to emulate, many of these children mature into adults who are poorly equipped to handle reality. They know gambling or drinking only as a means of stress relief, or as a way of having fun.

Cultural Factors

Culture significantly influences behavior. If a particular activity is valued in a culture, then the activity will be portrayed positively. This in turn encourages participation in the activity. In North America, this is generally the case with both gambling and alcohol consumption. Further, social acceptance, such as peer pressure, modeling influences, and so on, adds credibility to other reasons for gambling and drinking. Exposing individuals to gambling and drinking that is portrayed positively on television and in the movies enhances the attractiveness of the two activities.

In North America, gambling and alcohol consumption are generally accepted. Furthermore, because both activities are associated with being "grown up," children and teenagers tend look forward to engaging in them, in much the same way that they look forward to being able to drive a vehicle.

Exposure and Availability

It would be difficult to consume alcohol or to gamble, if the opportunities to do so were not available. Exposure to an activity that is readily available makes it easy to participate in the activity. In North America, and in many other parts of the world, individuals are continuously exposed to gambling and drinking. In most cases, both activities are portrayed in a positive manner. The exposure and the availability make gambling and drinking very popular.

Cognitive Expectations

Cognitive expectancy is defined as: "the thoughts people have with regard to the likely outcome or consequences of a given situation" (Jaffe and Lohse 1991). Cognitive expectations play a role in determining whether an individual will gamble or drink. Often, what an individual expects from an activity is as important to the outcome as the nature of the activity itself. For example, if gambling is portrayed as an enjoyable activity, then individuals will expect to have fun while gambling and therefore look forward to engaging in the activity. This in turn increases their chances of enjoying it. When people engage in an activity in response to peer pressure, it is usually because of positive peer representation of the activity. In the same manner, cognitive expectations influence drinking behavior. For example, if getting drunk is perceived as being positive, then people persuade themselves that they enjoy intoxication, even if the experience is not intrinsically pleasurable at first.

Self-Enhancement

Some people discover that gambling or drinking results in self-enhancement, in one form or another. For example, a shy woman has difficulty relating socially with others. She discovers that when she is under the influence of alcohol, she interacts more easily with people. A man with a negative self-concept discovers that a big win in gambling makes him the envy of the crowd. Others gamble or drink and discover that it relieves them of anxiety or depression. In other words, gambling and alcohol consumption can foster a sense of self-enhancement.

However, this sense of self-enhancement, whether real or an illusion, carries a significant drawback. When gambling or drinking become the chief means of relief or the vehicle to enhance performance, the individual is increasingly faced with the temptation, if not the need, to gamble or drink more frequently and for longer periods.

Desire to Win Money

In most cases, people gamble and consume alcohol for similar reasons. However, there is one reason why people gamble that does not apply to alcohol consumption. The hope of a big win. They dream of immediate riches. For those who have lost substantial amounts of money through gambling, the desire for a big win often becomes an obsession. They believe that winning is the only way to relieve them from the stress of their losses. In the case of alcohol consumption, there is no opportunity for a big financial win.

3
Types of Gamblers and Drinkers of Alcohol

Not all people who gamble or consume alcohol do so in the same manner. Different people drink and/or gamble in different ways. When one views the variety of ways in which people gamble or drink, various patterns emerge. For example, some may drink or gamble in ways that indicate that the behaviors are not significant parts of their lifestyles. For others, gambling and/or drinking is more central to their lifestyles. For some, gambling or drinking become so central to their existence that they believe they cannot function without one or the other, or, in some cases, both.

This chapter identifies and compares patterns of drinking and gambling. In my book (1989), I differentiate between three types of drinkers: social drinkers, problem drinkers, and alcoholics. Social drinkers may be further differentiated into light and regular drinkers. Custer and Milt (1985) describe different types of gamblers. Although there are some differences, parallels emerge between patterns of alcohol consumption and patterns of gambling.

Social Drinkers

The majority of individuals who consume alcohol are social drinkers. In my book (1989), I describe social drinkers as individuals who restrict their drinking to appropriate times and places and who know when to stop. They do not experience drinking-related problems, and, therefore, do not concern themselves with cutting back or quitting. Generally, social drinkers do not rely upon alcohol consumption as a tool to enhance performance (e.g., "I cannot dance unless I've had a few drinks.") or as a means of escape (e.g., "the only way I know how to relax is to drink."). During periods of stress or during situations requiring mental exertion, social drinkers tend to decrease their alcohol consumption, often without thinking about it. Usually, social drinkers consume alcohol because they like the taste, or because they enjoy drinking as part of social situations.

There are two types of social drinkers; occasional and regular. Occasional drinkers consume alcohol in response to particular occasions. For example, they may consume wine with certain meals, or have a few bottles of beer while watching a sporting event. For them, drinking is not a regular activity, but rather an activity linked to various situations or events. However, the occasional social drinker is not bothered by the absence of alcohol at these times. The occasional drinker does not give drinking priority over family, job, or other considerations.

By comparison, regular social drinkers consume alcohol on a relatively consistent basis. For example, some people have a drink when they come home from work, whereas others have a glass of wine with supper, and so on. Some regular social drinkers do not drink every day, but do so regularly on weekends. They may drink every Friday or

Saturday night. For regular social drinkers, alcohol consumption is more important than it is for occasional social drinkers. Even though alcohol consumption is a routine for them, regular drinkers do not allow drinking to interfere with other activities, and, like the occasional drinker, they place family, job, and various other activities above drinking.

In my book (1989), I describe several factors which differentiate social drinkers from other types of drinkers. Social drinkers:

- always control how much alcohol they consume. They never drink more than they intend. This is different from the individuals who intend to have a few drinks, but, instead, close down the bar. The latter is not social drinking.

- consume alcohol at appropriate times and places. Whether they are occasional or regular drinkers, these individuals restrict their consumption of alcohol to times when situations in which alcohol consumption does not interfere with, or impact negatively upon other activities. For example, social drinkers typically do not drink before going to work, while caring for children, or while engaging in activities that requires mental alertness and physical coordination.

- do not experience problems as a consequence of their drinking.

Case Example

Mary is a 30-year-old lawyer who works hard at her profession. When she comes home from work, she pours herself an ounce of Scotch. She kicks off her shoes, sinks into a comfortable chair, and sips her drink while reading the newspaper. On weekends, if Mary goes to a party or out for supper, she has a few drinks. During the week, Mary rarely has more than her daily ounce of Scotch. Mary doesn't drink on Sunday nights, or more than her pattern during the week, because she wants to be alert for work the next morning.

Case Example

Terry is an electrician who is married, with two young children. As a pastime, he enjoys weight-lifting. He also enjoys the taste of beer, and, here and there, he consumes a few bottles. Terry usually has his beer when he is out with his wife and their friends or after work with his buddies. This usually happens about once or twice a week, although sometimes Terry goes for several weeks without consuming alcohol. Although Terry usually maintains his consumption between two to four bottles of beer per occasion, sometimes he chooses to drink more heavily, and becomes mildly intoxicated. When Terry does change his pattern, it is usually on a Friday or Saturday night and never on an evening prior to work. Even though he enjoys drinking, Terry places it secondary to his family and his weight-lifting. He does not allow drinking to interfere with any of his activities with his children and his wife, or with his weight-lifting.

Both of these are examples of individuals who are social drinkers. Mary is a regular social drinker, and Terry is more of an occasional drinker. Neither individual consumes alcohol in a manner that impacts negatively upon work or other activities. Both of these people meet the criteria defining social drinking, in that they are in control of how much alcohol they consume, and they drink at times and in situations where it is appropriate to do so. For both, drinking does not interfere with other aspects of their functioning. In other words, these two individuals are in control of their alcohol consumption, rather than allowing their alcohol consumption to control them.

Case Example

Edward is a 52-year-old married man, whose children are grown and living away from home. Whenever Edward comes home from work, he feels that he must have a couple of drinks. If he does not have his alcohol, he is moody and irritable. Whenever Edward is in a social situation, he is uncomfortable, unless alcohol is available. If he is to attend an event where alcohol is not served, Edward fortifies himself with a few drinks. On several occasions, while attending social events, Edward has had a few too many drinks. Once, he insulted his wife in front of their friends, and acted rudely toward others. Sometimes, after drinking fairly heavily the evening before, Edward has attended work, hung-over and smelling noticeably of alcohol. Also, there are times when Edward's drinking has resulted in arguments with his wife.

If one were to ask Edward about his drinking, he would adamantly claim that he is a social drinker, and that he does not have a problem with alcohol. However, Edward's pattern of alcohol consumption is inconsistent with that of social drinking. First, Edward needs to consume alcohol in order to feel comfortable, and he is irritable and moody when does not have it. Second, Edward fortifies himself with alcohol, prior to attending events where he cannot drink. Third, he has, on occasion, drank too much, and while under the influence, Edward has acted inappropriately. Fourth, Edward has turned up at work hung-over. Fifth, Edward's drinking has resulted in arguments between he and his wife. In other words, Edward's alcohol consumption is interfering with his marriage and with his work. Edward is not in control of his drinking. It is controlling him.

Problem Drinking

Problem drinkers are individuals who are potentially in control of their alcohol consumption, but who frequently allow themselves to drink excessively and in a fashion that causes problems. The major characteristic that separates problem drinkers from alcoholics is, problem drinkers are potentially able to control how much they consume, as well as when and where. In other words, problem drinkers are able to moderate their consumption to become social drinkers.

Case Example

Sandy is a fourth-year university student. Her goal is to attend graduate school and become a social worker. On weekends, Sandy liked to party. Invariably on both Friday and Saturday nights, Sandy drank excessively and became very intoxicated. Because of this, she was not able to study effectively on weekends. During the week, Sandy would sometimes go to a pub with friends and become intoxicated. This resulted in her missing classes and along with poor study habits, caused Sandy's marks to drop.

For several months, Sandy dated a fellow who consumed alcohol infrequently and lightly. Because Sandy liked him, she moderated her drinking pattern to approximate his. However, when the relationship broke up, Sandy resumed her heavy drinking.

At some point Sandy realized that unless she applied herself, she would not be admitted to graduate school. Sandy promised herself two things; first, she would spend considerably more time studying and, second, she would consume considerably less alcohol. Studying more, and drinking less, Sandy significantly improved her academic performance.

Sandy is an example of a problem drinker. Her style of heavy alcohol consumption was impacting her studies in a harmful manner. However, Sandy was able to moderate and maintain her alcohol consumption, such that she now drinks in a manner that is not harmful.

It is not too difficult to differentiate between social drinking and alcoholism. However, it is considerably more difficult to determine if a person is a problem drinker, as opposed to an alcoholic. The main difference is, problem drinkers are able to control their consumption, such that they may chose moderation. On the other hand, alcoholics are individuals who have reached a stage in their consumption of alcohol at which attempts at moderation are futile. An alcoholic's only viable choice, is to stop drinking entirely.

Gambling

There are obvious parallels between particular patterns of gambling and patterns of alcohol consumption. However, some patterns of gambling have no equivalent, with regard to alcohol consumption. Custer and Milt (1985) identify six types of gamblers. These are: the casual social gambler, the serious social gambler, the professional gambler, the antisocial or criminal gambler, the relief and escape gambler, and the compulsive gambler (now referred to as the pathological gambler).

Casual Social Gambler

The casual social gambler is an individual who gambles for recreation, enjoyment, and excitement. However, gambling is not a central part of this individual's lifestyle. The casual gambler likes to win, but losses are not considered serious, because typically, they are not significant. This person gambles for fun, and losses are considered the cost of the entertainment. The casual social gambler controls how much he or she gambles and always knows when to leave a gambling situation. Gambling is not placed before family, work, friends, and other important activities. Casual social gambling is comparable to social drinking, in that neither activity is harmful.

Serious Social Gambler

To the serious social gambler, gambling is more important than it is to the casual gambler. Serious social gamblers invest more of themselves into gambling. They gamble more regularly, spend more money on gambling, and, for them, gambling is a main form of recreation. However, serious social gamblers still give priority to their families and work. Although occasional conflicts may arise between the gambler and family members over how much money is spent on gambling, there is no apparent loss of control over gambling. Like regular social drinkers who control their consumption of alcohol, serious social gamblers are able to moderate how much they gamble.

Case Example

Lawrence enjoys the occasional card game with his friends but not enough to play regularly. He plays about six times a year or so, mainly if he is invited, and if he has nothing else to do. Lawrence plays cards to socialize, as opposed to win money. If he happens to leave a game with a few extra dollars, he perceives it as a bonus. Alternatively, if Lawrence loses a few dollars, he perceives this as the cost of enjoyment. Generally, Lawrence and his friends gamble for low stakes.

Besides the occasional game of cards, Lawrence and his wife visit Las Vegas once every two years. They usually go with friends. While in Las Vegas, Lawrence and his wife spend several hours each day playing the slot machines, and blackjack. They also like to spend time at the hotel pool, watch the shows, and go out for nice dinners. They always have a limit as to how much money they are prepared to lose, and if Lawrence and his wife reach their limit, they stop gambling. They include their limit as part of the cost of the trip. If they happen to win, they see this as a bonus.

Lawrence is a casual social gambler. He gambles occasionally, and when he does, it is usually part of a greater social context. He is in control of how much he gambles, and gambles at appropriate times and places. Gambling is not central to Lawrence's lifestyle, and further, gambling is not a high priority.

Case Example

Frank will admit that he enjoys gambling, especially at the horse races. During racing season, Frank attends the horse races with his two friends, every Friday evening. This is a weekly ritual for Frank. Sometimes, Frank's wife will go with him. She has however come to accept that, during the racing season, Frank will be at the races on Friday evenings. Last year, the times that Frank did not go to the races where when his parents celebrated their fiftieth wedding anniversary party and when his daughter graduated from university.

Even though Frank loves the races, he limits how much he will spend. Also, if Frank does not like the horses in a particular race, he will not bet. Winning does not prompt further gambling by Frank, and losses do not exceed a preset limit.

Frank is a serious social gambler. He considers gambling to be an important form of recreation and, from an emotional perspective, invests more of himself than does Lawrence. While Lawrence can take gambling or leave it, gambling is for Frank, the central component to enjoying a Friday evening. Despite this, Frank still places his family before his gambling. If an important family event occurs, Frank will give it priority over gambling.

Both casual social gambling and serious social gambling may be compared to social drinking. Casual gambling is akin to occasional social drinking, and serious social gambling is comparable to regular social drinking. In all cases, whether it is gambling or drinking, the individual is in control. Neither gambling nor drinking has priority over family, occupation, and other important obligations.

The Professional Gambler

For the professional gambler, gambling is an occupation. These people make their living by gambling. They develop a high level of skill at the games they choose to play, in the same manner that other individuals develop skill at their jobs. These gamblers are very much in control of how much money they bet, and they know when to walk away if they are losing. Further, they lead a balanced lifestyle, placing importance upon their family, friends, and financial security. Generally, professional gamblers do not like to gamble as a leisure activity. For them, gambling is work. Examples of professional gamblers include professional card players and stock market investors (especially those who invest in higher-risk ventures).

With respect to alcohol consumption, there does not appear to be an equivalent to the professional gambler, except perhaps the professional wine taster.

The Antisocial or Criminal Gambler

This type of gambler does not have a problem with gambling, *per se.* Rather, the antisocial gambler uses gambling as a vehicle to cheat or swindle others. These people typically have a history of illegal activities and other types of problem behavior, including an inability to sustain meaningful relationships, poor academic performance, and a history of having been fired from or leaving jobs. Sometimes, the antisocial gambler will use the excuse of a gambling problem, as a defense in court, when in reality a gambling problem does not exist.

Similarly, some people who do not have a problem with alcohol may use drinking as an excuse for criminal activity. However, there are also people who have a problem with alcohol and who commit criminal offenses while under the influence. In many cases, these offenses would have not occurred, had the individual not been under the influence of alcohol. In a parallel manner, some individuals who have a problem with gambling, feel compelled to commit criminal offenses, to acquire funds with which to pay off their overwhelming debts. Consequently, it is important to differentiate between people who rely upon the excuse of drinking or gambling as a (legal) defense against criminal charges, and those individuals who have drinking or gambling problems.

The Relief-and-Escape Gambler

The fifth type of gambler that Custer and Milt describe is the relief-and-escape gambler. This individual relies upon gambling as a source of relief from unpleasant emotions or as a vehicle to escape unpleasant situations. Because of its significant avoidance component, this type of gambling has pathological elements. Instead of dealing with uncomfortable emotions, the individual relies upon gambling as a method of relief.

The relief-and-escape gambler gambles not for enjoyment or excitement, but rather to reduce or eliminate uncomfortable feelings. The relief and escape gambler may be compared to the problem drinker who uses alcohol as a means of escape or emotional relief. The gambling pattern of the relief and escape gambler is often characterized by binges. Uncomfortable emotions build, and the individual gambles for relief.

Case Example

Faye is a 48-year-old housewife. She and her husband have been married for 25 years, and they have two children who are living away from home and successful in their careers. Faye loves her husband, and, if asked, she will claim that she is content in her marriage. Prior to having had children, Faye worked in a bank. She enjoyed her work. However, prior to giving birth to her first child, Faye made the decision to resign from her position at the bank, in order to raise her child, and later her second child. Faye's husband supported her decision, although he would have supported Faye, had she decided otherwise.

While the children were young, Faye was a devoted mother, and her days were meaningful. However, as her children grew and matured and no longer needed their mother, Faye became solitary and depressed. One day, on her way to shop for food, Faye decided to go into a local casino that had just opened. She had heard much about the casino, and she wanted to see what the excitement was all about. Faye tried the slot machines, and before she knew it, she was relieved of the boredom and feeling useless.

At first, Faye restricted her gambling to once a week, for about an hour or so. However, within a short time, Faye was gambling frequently and for extended periods. She gambles most when her husband is on business trips; times when her depression and loneliness peak.

Once or twice a year, Faye and her husband go on vacation. Faye loves these times, because she enjoys being with her husband, and she relishes his undivided attention.

Even though there are casinos at places where Faye and her husband vacation, Faye has no desire to gamble.

Faye is a relief-and-escape gambler. When she is neither lonely nor depressed, Faye has no desire to gamble. However, when Faye is bored, depressed, and lonely, gambling provides relief.

Like the problem drinker who is at risk to developing alcoholism, the relief-and-escape gambler is at risk to developing pathological gambling. The following chapters deal with these two disorders.

4
What is an Addiction?

An individual is addicted to an activity or a substance when that person cannot control the extent to which he or she engages in the activity or how much of the substance he or she consumes. An individual is also considered addicted when he or she continues to engage in the activity or to use a substance, despite obvious harmful consequences. As well, addiction is typically characterized by a withdrawal reaction, when the activity, or use of the substance, is suddenly discontinued.

There are several components to an addiction. All addictions have a powerful psychological component, and many have a physical component that varies in intensity across substances. Further, all addictions, unless they are arrested in time, result in social deterioration for the addicted person. The words addiction and dependence are often used synonymously and are used so in this text.

Psychological Dependence

Psychological dependence to an activity or a substance occurs when the activity or the substance is central to an individual's thoughts and emotions. An addicted person is often preoccupied with thoughts of engaging in the activity or the use of the substance. If a person needs to engage in an activity or to use a substance, despite potentially harmful consequences, psychological dependence exists.

Many individuals who are psychologically dependent cannot wait to complete their day-to-day duties, in order that they may engage in their desired activity or use their desired substance. Often, a psychological addiction is so overwhelming that individuals will allow it to interfere with other important activities, such as spending time with family or friends, going to school, or working. Unless they are engaging in the desired activity, or under the influence of a substance, severely addicted people feel emotionally vulnerable. They also feel significant discomfort and, occasionally, panic, if they are prevented from engaging in the activity or using the substance.

Despite long-term harmful consequences, people continue to engage in their addiction habit, because they experience immediate positive consequences, usually in the form of very pleasant feelings or relief from discomfort. In other words, psychologically dependent people opt for immediate gratification, despite potentially harmful long-term consequences.

The longer a individual engages in an addiction, the greater the psychological adaptation. In other words, to realize emotional gratification, the individual requires increasingly greater amounts of the substance or activity.

Physical Dependence

So far, there is no definitive evidence to suggest that individuals may become physically dependent upon activities that do not involve the ingestion of a substance. However, there is evidence that people may become physically dependent upon certain substances.

Physical dependence to a substance is characterized by two processes: an increase in tolerance and a withdrawal reaction. Increased tolerance to a substance occurs when the body physically adapts to the presence of a substance, such that increasingly greater amounts are required to produce the same effects that lesser amounts used to produce. In other words, physical addictions are often characterized by a history reflecting increasingly greater amounts of consumption.

A withdrawal or detoxification reaction occurs when an individual who is addicted to a substance abruptly stops using the substance. Because the person's body has physically adapted to the presence of the substance, a sudden absence of the substance results in acute distress. To avoid the discomfort of withdrawal, addicted individuals feel compelled to maintain their intake of the substance (or substances, as the case may be). However, many people not only maintain their intake to avoid going into withdrawal, but many, because of tolerance, must consume increasingly greater amounts of the substance to achieve the sought-after effects. This occasionally leads to a potentially life-threatening overdose.

Social Features of an Addiction

Addictions usually manifest themselves through social disruption. This is most evident in the families of actively addicted individuals. Typically, these families are characterized by discord, dissension, emotional distress, and arguments. Unless the addiction is arrested, family breakdown is almost inevitable.

Addictions also result in a breakdown in friendships. Because the addiction eventually gains priority over every-thing else, including friendships, the addicted individual ex-periences a loss of interest in non-using friends. People who are active in their addictions (as opposed to an addiction that has been arrested) usually only voluntarily associate with those, who are similarly addicted. Because severe ad-dictions usually supersede everything, unless the addiction is arrested, the addicted person typically ends up alone.

Addictions result in a loss of interest in activities, other than those pertaining to the addiction. Even when en-gaged with other things, most addicts cannot wait to finish, so that they may resume their addictive behavior. Some people cannot wait. They'll partake in their addiction, even when engaging in other activities such as caring for their children, working, or while attending school. Consequently, poor parenting, and poor academic and vocational perform-ance are characteristic of addictions.

Addictions and financial problems usually go hand-in-hand. For maintenance, most addictions require money. Addicts quickly learn that any interruption to their addic-tion, will result in feelings of significant discomfort. Conse-quently, they spend whatever is required to keep their addiction alive. This usually involves giving their addiction financial priority over caring for their families, buying food and clothing, paying bills, etc. Some people take on extra jobs, borrow money, sell personal belongings, or engage in criminal activity in order to obtain funds.

Because addicted individuals tend to perform poorly at school or at work, many end up dropping out of or being expelled from school, quitting their jobs, or being fired. Many also lose their families. This, in concert with spending most of their money maintaining their addiction, results in social deterioration. The criminal activity of many addicts results in arrests. Many also face legal problems associated with bankruptcy and divorce. Experiencing multiple losses, many addicts develop severe depressions, and some attempt suicide.

Common Features of all Addictions

All addictions have common features. All addicts, regardless of the nature of their addiction, maintain their addictive behavior despite obvious harmful consequences. They opt for the immediate pleasurable effects of their addictive behavior and ignore the long-term potential harm. Consequently, all addictions are characterized by progressive psychological, physical, and social deterioration. Even though various addictions share common features, research has not revealed significant evidence of an addiction-prone personality type (Walters 1994). In other words, it does not appear that a particular personality type will specifically lead to the development of an addiction. There are however, specific factors that render certain individuals more prone than others to developing an addiction. These factors are reviewed later.

5
Alcoholism

What is Alcoholism?

Alcoholism is an addiction to alcohol. What separates an alcoholic from other types of drinkers is that alcoholics have difficulty controlling how much alcohol they consume. Some alcoholics are daily drinkers, and others are periodic drinkers. Regardless of frequency of consumption, once an alcoholic begins drinking, that individual usually drinks to excess. Even when the alcoholic tries to control consumption, the effort is usually futile.

Besides not being able to control how much they drink, alcoholics often drink at inappropriate times and places. The addiction controls the alcoholic. By comparison, social drinkers do not drink more than they intend, and when they drink, they restrict their consumption to proper times and places.

The difference between problem drinkers and alcoholics is that, even though problem drinkers sometimes experience problems secondary to their alcohol intake, these drinkers are potentially able to moderate and control their alcohol consumption; alcoholics, for the most part, cannot. When alcoholics attempt to moderate their intake, they are usually only temporarily successful. They may control their drinking for days, weeks, or sometimes even months, but sooner or later heavy drinking resumes. Like other drug addictions, the alcoholic's only realistic choice is to stop drinking entirely. To continue drinking involves the risk of progressive deterioration.

Criteria for Addiction

Alcoholism is characterized by all of the criteria for substance dependence or addiction, as defined by the Diagnostic and Statistical Manual of Mental Disorders (fourth edition) of the American Psychiatric Association (1994, p.181). These criteria are a breakdown of the general themes of addiction, described in the previous chapter.

According to the D.S.M. IV, one indicator of an addiction to a substance is, an increase in tolerance evidenced by a need to consume increasingly greater quantities of the substance to achieve a desired effect. Alcoholics historically must consume increasingly greater quantities of alcohol to produce the same effects previously produced by lesser quantities. Whereas smaller amounts of alcohol used to make an individual drunk, now only large quantities will suffice. Consequently, the ability to hold one's liquor is not a sign of accomplishment. Instead, "holding one's liquor" is an indication of possible or impending alcoholism.

A second criterion of addiction is a withdrawal reaction, which occurs when the individual stops taking the substance. Often, the same substance is taken to relieve or prevent a withdrawal reaction. Whenever alcoholics stop drinking, most experience a withdrawal or detoxification reaction, as it is often called. Withdrawal symptoms include anxiety, perspiring, tremors (the "shakes"), and in severe cases, convulsive seizures. Some alcoholics in severe withdrawal may experience Alcohol Withdrawal Delirium (D.S.M. IV 1994); a condition characterized by visual, tactile and auditory hallucinations (they see, feel, or hear things that are not really there). Sometimes, the hallucinations are frightening to the individual and may result in acts of self-harm. Alcoholics learn that they can prevent a withdrawal reaction if they resume drinking.

A third characteristic of substance dependence is that the substance is taken in greater amounts and for longer periods than is intended. This loss of control over consumption is a consistent feature of alcoholism.

The D.S.M. IV also states that individuals who are addicted to a substance will often show repeated, albeit unsuccessful, efforts to cut down or to control their use of the substance. Alcoholics often attempt to control their intake, but they are usually unsuccessful.

Another characteristic of substance dependence, and specifically alcoholism, includes spending a great deal of time obtaining and using the substance. This certainly applies to alcoholism. Further, alcoholics spend large amounts of money to purchase alcohol, and they give their alcohol consumption priority over important activities. Many people lose jobs, friendships, and their families, as a consequence of their drinking.

A major feature of substance dependence, including dependence upon alcohol, is the continued use of the substance, despite persistent and recurrent harmful consequences. Alcoholics continue to drink, even though drinking causes physical, psychological, and social problems for them.

A common symptom specific to alcoholism, but not necessarily to other addictive substances, is alcohol-induced bouts of temporary amnesia, or blackouts, as they are called. A bout of temporary amnesia is a period of time in which an individual who is or recently had been drinking experiences no recall. The person has no recollection of what he or she had said or done. While under the influence of alcohol and in a blackout, some individuals engage in embarrassing, violent, or criminal behaviors. When they become sober, they have no recall of what had transpired. Blackouts may range in length from a few minutes to several days. The typical blackout lasts several hours.

Case Example

Howard began drinking as a teen-ager. During these years, Howard restricted his alcohol consumption to weekends, mainly Friday and Saturday evenings. However, Howard always drank to significant intoxication.

By the time Howard was in his twenties, he was drinking more frequently — on weekends and after work. To reach his desired level of intoxication, Howard had to consume considerably more alcohol than he used to. Consequently, he developed a reputation for being able to hold his liquor, a condition that certainly gave Howard bragging rights.

Despite a significant increase in his alcohol consumption, Howard would sometimes go to a bar or a pub with the intent of just having a few drinks and not getting drunk. Regardless of his intentions, Howard became intoxicated. As a result, he sometimes came late for work the next day, or even missed work. Occasionally, Howard's drinking would extend well into the next day. On a few occasions, Howard's benders lasted for several days. After benders, Howard felt sick to his stomach, nervous, he perspired excessively, and he was tremulous. However, a few drinks usually eliminated the discomfort. When he drank, Howard sometimes experienced blackouts. One evening while in a blackout, Howard provoked a fist fight. He was subsequently arrested for assault. The next day, Howard could not believe what had happened. He had no recollection of what had transpired the previous evening.

Despite obvious problems, Howard persisted in drinking. He eventually lost his job, and his response was to go on a bender, which lasted well over a week.

Howard shows typical symptoms of alcoholism. When he consumes alcohol, Howard loses control over how much he drinks, and he becomes significantly intoxicated. Howard also requires greater amounts of alcohol to reach his desired level of intoxication. He has withdrawal reactions after bouts of heavy drinking, and he persists in consuming alcohol, despite obvious harmful consequences.

6
Pathological Gambling

According to Rosenthal (1992), the term pathological gambling was given official recognition by the Diagnostic and Statistical Manual, third edition (1980), of the American Psychiatric Association. This term was recognized as being more accurate than the term compulsive gambling, which had been used previously. The D.S.M. III, revised edition (1987) recognized pathological gambling as a disorder similar to alcoholism.

Rosenthal (1992, p.72) defines pathological gambling as "a progressive disorder characterized by a continuous or periodic loss of control over gambling; a preoccupation with gambling and with obtaining money with which to gamble; irrational thinking; and a continuation of the behavior despite adverse consequences." Rosenthal goes on to draw a parallel between pathological gambling and substance dependence, including alcoholism.

Custer and Milt (1985) state that pathological gambling has four essential elements. One is progression. Once pathological gamblers begin gambling, they have trouble stopping. They cannot quit when they are ahead. Consequently, they experience progressively greater losses. Pathological gamblers, always expecting the "big win," increase the size of their bets and spend increasing amounts of time gambling. Given the odds, they lose more than they win, and their situation progressively worsens.

The second element of pathological gambling is the intolerance of losing. While social gamblers view losing as the cost of the entertainment, and professional gamblers view losses as the cost of doing business, the pathological gambler personalizes losses. Rather than being accepted as a component of gambling, losses are perceived as an assault on self-esteem. When they are winning, pathological gamblers feel good about themselves — the reverse is true, when they are losing. By contrast, social and professional gamblers do not value themselves as a function of wins and losses. Also, because they are in control of their gambling, social and professional gamblers do not experience the severe losses characteristic of pathological gambling. Because pathological gamblers are intolerant of losses, and because their style of gambling allows for large losses, these gamblers feel compelled to *chase* their money. In other words, they become obsessed with gambling to recoup their losses. However, the odds dictate that chasing doesn't work. Further losses create panic, and any rational strategy that the pathological gambler may have previously employed, is abandoned.

The third characteristic described by Custer and Milt is the preoccupation with gambling. The pathological gambler is constantly preoccupied with thoughts of gambling. The individual cannot wait to complete nongambling activities, so that he or she may gamble. In the mind of this type of gambler, gambling comes to assume greater importance than it deserves. The gambler is convinced that gambling is not only a way to solve financial problems, but also other living problems. With time, the pathological gambler loses rational perspective and focuses upon gambling.

The last feature of pathological gambling is the continuation of gambling without regard for harmful consequences. Obsessed by thoughts of winning, the pathological gambler persists in gambling, regardless of the outcome. If the individual does by chance win a large amount of money, this strengthens the gambler's grandiose belief that more big wins are just around the corner. Usually, the odds prevail, and losses overshadow wins.

Grandiose thinking, which is so characteristic of the pathological gambler, causes the gambler to abandon moral and ethical values, thus opening the door for illegal activities, such as, for example, theft and forgery. Fear of being caught coerces the individual into gambling more, under the belief that a big win will rectify the situation.

The difference between the relief-and-escape gambler and the pathological gambler is that the former is able to control his or her gambling, whereas the latter cannot. Although gambling for unhealthy reasons, the relief and escape gambler does manage to avoid the harmful downward spiral, so characteristic of the pathological gambler.

Pathological Gambling and Alcoholism

Pathological gambling is very similar to alcoholism. Both disorders are characterized by progressive deterioration. As a result of their disorders, alcoholics and pathological gamblers amass problems, and both unrealistically rely upon their respective habits to provide relief, thus strengthening the downward spiral.

The pathological gambler develops an intolerance to losing and becomes obsessed with winning to recoup losses. The alcoholic develops an intolerance of abstinence, and becomes obsessed with drinking as a means of relief. Both addicts believe that they cannot function effectively, without their respective gambling or drinking.

Pathological gamblers have a preoccupation with gambling, akin to an alcoholic's preoccupation with drinking. Thoughts of either gambling or drinking are forever present. Both give their habits priority over family, friends, job, school, and other activities. This is evidenced by the fact, that both pathological gamblers and alcoholics partake in their respective habits, with a notable disregard for the harmful consequences.

D.S.M. IV Criteria for Pathological Gambling

The D.S.M. IV criteria for pathological gambling and for substance dependence, including alcoholism, are remarkably similar. However, despite this similarity, the D.S.M. IV (p. 609) classifies pathological gambling as an Impulse Control Disorder Not Elsewhere Classified.

For all impulse-control disorders, the afflicted individual experiences an increase in tension prior to acting out the disorder and tension relief, pleasure, or gratification while committing the act, or just after the act. Pathological gambling shows some of the characteristics of an impulse control disorder, in that some pathological gamblers experience an uncomfortable tension that is relieved through gambling. However, most pathological gamblers do not experience relief after the act of gambling, especially if they lose. Rather, they feel irritable and restless and typically only quit gambling due to time constraints (sometimes), exhaustion, or running out of money. For them, relief from tension is usually restricted to the act of gambling. In the more chronic stages of pathological gambling, anxiety, irritability, and panic are common, even while gambling. For the chronic gambler, relief from tension is remote. Consequently, despite some similarities to disorders of impulse control, pathological gambling appears more closely related to alcoholism (and other types of substance dependence). Further, the D.S.M. IV criteria for pathological gambling very closely resemble those for substance dependence, including alcoholism.

The first criterion for pathological gambling is the individual's preoccupation with gambling, a preoccupation that parallels the alcoholic's preoccupation with alcohol. In the majority of cases, when pathological gamblers are not gambling, they are thinking about it. If they're not thinking about gambling, they're thinking about ways of acquiring money with which to gamble. The same holds true for alcoholics and their alcohol.

The second criterion is the gambler's need to gamble with increasingly greater amounts of money. The pathological gambler finds that larger bets are now needed to produce the same level of excitement that smaller bets used to. This is very much like the alcoholic's increase in tolerance to alcohol.

The third criterion is a history of unsuccessful efforts to control, moderate, or stop gambling; a process not unlike an alcoholic's history of unsuccessful attempts at moderation or quitting alcohol consumption.

The fourth criterion is evidence of irritability, after the individual attempts to cut down or quit gambling. When a pathological gambler attempts to quit or even moderate his or her gambling, the individual feels uncomfortable. This discomfort, which is usually relieved with further gambling, is akin to the withdrawal syndrome of the alcoholic; a syndrome that is eliminated through further drinking.

The fifth criterion of pathological gambling is the use of gambling as a means of relief or escape from uncomfortable emotions and problems. Gambling relieves the individual of guilt, anxiety, depression, and a host of other uncomfortable emotions. Alcoholics consume alcohol for the same reasons. For both, the relief effect is only temporary and is followed by more discomfort.

Chasing one's losses is another characteristic of pathological gamblers. This occurs when the pathological gambler, after a loss, feels compelled to return and recoup the loss. Chasing (losses) is a behavior that parallels the alcoholic drinking to avoid a withdrawal reaction.

Other criteria of pathological gambling include lying to others, committing illegal acts, jeopardizing relationships, and so on. This too is characteristic of alcoholism. The gambler's attempt to convince others to bail him or her out of various predicaments (another criterion) is similar to the enabling of the alcoholic; the protecting of the alcoholic from the harmful consequences of drinking.

Case Example

Janice works as a payroll clerk for a large company. She is married and has two children, both living away from home. Janice's husband is a successful commodities broker.

Janice began gambling about five years ago. At first, Janice liked to play bingo. She went with a couple of her girlfriends, about once or twice a week. Janice's husband encouraged her to go, believing that she needed a night or two out with her friends. Besides, her husband enjoyed playing cards with his friends on one of the evenings that Janice was out; on the other evening he took cooking classes.

About two years ago, Janice experimented with the slot machines. She immediately discovered that the slots were more exciting than bingo, and further, she could go alone, whereas bingo was boring unless friends were along. On a few occasions, Janice was lucky and had big wins. Once she won over a thousand dollars. Spurred on by her wins, Janice delved into playing the slots. She also switched to machines that allowed her to increase the size of her bets.

Besides gambling more often and with larger bets, Janice found herself thinking a lot about gambling and talking about it. However, despite a few big wins, Janice was losing more than she was winning. Before she knew it, Janice was dipping into her bank account for money with which to gamble. When Janice's husband expressed concern about their decreasing balance, she lied about costly car repairs.

During this last year, Janice has been gambling almost daily. She goes after work, often coming home late for supper. She lies to her husband, telling him that she is working late. Losing money, Janice is now borrowing from her coworkers, with promises to pay them back. She is also panicking over her losses, feeling an irresistible urge to gamble, to win back her lost money.

When Janice is at home, she is irritable and often angry. Her husband senses that something is wrong, but whenever he approaches Janice with his concerns, he is accused of prying.

Janice is a pathological gambler. Rather than being in control of how much Janice gambles, the gambling controls her. Janice gambles more frequently and with larger bets. Janice is uncomfortable when she is not gambling, obsessed with chasing her losses, indebted to fellow workers, and she lies to her husband to cover her gambling.

When the D.S.M. IV diagnostic criteria for substance dependence and, specifically, alcoholism are compared with those for pathological gambling, the similarities are obvious. Both alcoholics and pathological gamblers are out of control with respect to their disorders, and this loss of control generalizes to many aspects of their lives. Given the strong similarities between the two disorders, a case can be made that pathological gambling is very addiction-like and more closely resembles substance dependence, than it does impulse-control disorders. Shaffer (1996) makes the point that physical dependence is not necessary for the occurrence of an addiction. He believes that the concept of addiction applies to both substances and activities. Shaffer goes on to say that, if addiction can occur either with or without physical dependence, then any activity or substance that significantly affects "subjective experience," is potentially addictive. Gambling certainly impacts, in a significant manner, the subjective experiences of many people.

Multiple Addiction

It is not uncommon for individuals to be multiply addicted. For example, in my book (1995), I described how many cocaine addicts and other substance abusers are also alcoholics. Clinical evidence also indicates that many addicts have problems with both alcoholism and pathological gambling. Jacobs, Elia, and Goldstein (1991) found that, among 1700 patients in alcohol- and drug-treatment programs in V.A. hospitals, 14 percent were pathological gamblers. Sixteen percent more were problem gamblers at risk to becoming pathological gamblers. Another study (Lesieur, Blume, and Zoppa 1986) found that among 458 inpatient alcoholic and drug abusers, 9 percent were pathological gamblers and another 10 percent were high-risk. In both studies, the South Oaks Gambling Screen was utilized to assess pathological gambling. This instrument is both reliable and valid (Lesieur and Blume 1987).

Ciarrocchi (1993) found that among substance abusers, the rates of both pathological and problem gambling are two-and-a-half times greater than the general population. Conversely, some studies of pathological gamblers in treatment, found that about half had problems with either alcohol or other drug abuse (Ramirez, McCormick, Russo et al. 1984; Lesieur 1988).

7
Indicators of Pathological Gambling and Alcoholism

The two previous chapters present the diagnostic criteria and characteristics of alcoholism and pathological gambling. Because individuals with either disorder behave so similarly, the indicators for both are similar. This chapter presents behavior patterns that are indicative of pathological gambling and of alcoholism.

Time Spent Gambling or Drinking

The more time that an individual spends either drinking or gambling increases the probability that a problem exists. Because social drinkers and social gamblers do not give their respective activities priority over family, job, or other important commitments, and because other recreational pursuits are also important to these individuals, there is not a substantial amount of time allocated to either drinking or gambling. Even with regular social drinkers and serious social gamblers, the time spent engaged in either activity is restricted. However, because alcoholics and pathological gamblers give their respective habits priority over most other activities, and priority over everything, in the chronic stages of the disorders, drinking and/or gambling consume substantial amounts of time. Regardless, the amount of time an individual spends gambling is not in itself a completely reliable indicator that a problem may exist. For example, professional gamblers spend much time either gambling or planning their gambling. Therefore, the amount of time spent on gambling is significant only when other signs are also present. In the case of alcohol consumption, there is no common equivalent to the professional gambler. For example, compared to professional gamblers (stock brokers, commodities brokers, professional betters, etc.), professional wine tasters are relatively rare. Typically, when a lot of time is spent drinking, that time is a good indicator that a problem exists.

Increases in Gambling or Drinking

If a person shows a consistent increase in the time spent on gambling or drinking or in the amount of alcohol consumed or the size of bets, a problem may exist. Any increase in these behaviors may reflect a loss of control. Furthermore, if someone talks more and more about gambling or drinking, appears preoccupied with either activity, or looks for more ways to engage in one or the other, this suggests that a problem is brewing. One of the surest signs, is when an individual consistently seeks out places to either drink or gamble and resists alternatives when one or the other is not available. In other words, gambling or drinking are more important than other activities and interests. The person may also become annoyed at or show disinterest in people who do not wish to gamble or drink.

When individuals brag about either their gambling or their drinking, a problem may exist. In the case of gambling, if an individual always boasts about wins and avoids talking about losses, this may indicate that the person is too emotionally involved with gambling, is developing an unrealistic attitude about winning, and may be ignoring potential problems. Some pathological gamblers will even spend some of their winnings in a frivolous and show-off manner, which usually indicates a need to impress upon others that gambling is indeed beneficial and, therefore, not a problem. In the case of drinking, bragging about how much alcohol one consumes may be an indication that tolerance to alcohol has developed, thus indicating the presence of alcoholism.

Promises to Moderate or Quit

Alcoholics and pathological gamblers often promise that they'll either moderate or quit their respective habits. If individuals do not experience problems in response to their consumption of alcohol or to their gambling, they have no need to concern themselves with either moderation or abstinence. Further, they feel no need to make promises to do so. Consequently, promises to cut back or to quit are almost always indicative of problems, and always so, if the individual is unsuccessful in following through with the promise.

Financial and/or Legal Problems

If an individual is in financial or legal difficulty, and if there is ample evidence of gambling or alcohol consumption, there may be a relationship. Although there may be many reasons for financial or legal troubles, the chances are significant that alcoholics and pathological gamblers will experience problems in these areas.

Aberrations in Mood

Unexplainable aberrations in mood may be indicative of either alcoholism or pathological gambling. Although mood swings, anger, low tolerance for stress, irritability, anxiety, and depressions may be caused by a variety of other factors, they are also symptomatic of alcoholism and pathological gambling. Because both disorders create distress, this stress is adversely reflected in the mood of either the drinker or the gambler.

Drinking or Gambling in Response to Distress

Consistently engaging in alcohol consumption or gambling when stressed is another indicator that the individual has a problem with either. Whenever an individual uses either gambling or drinking as a tool to eliminate or reduce discomfort, the potential for dependence is significant.

Using Gambling or Drinking
as the Only Method for Enjoyment

Some individuals believe that they cannot enjoy themselves without gambling or drinking. Believing that no viable alternatives exist, they either drink or gamble (or both) to enjoy themselves. The potential danger is, if people associate only gambling or drinking with having fun, they come to resist accepting that either activity may cause problems. Therefore, they become less sensitive to the problems that do occur. These individuals tend to ignore early warning signs, thus placing themselves at risk to developing a dependence.

Hiding One's Gambling or Drinking

Another reliable indicator of either pathological gambling or alcoholism shows itself when an individual attempts to hide either activity. When people believe that they function well only when they are under the influence of alcohol or if they are gambling, they protect that belief through secrecy. Afraid of being found out and challenged, they lie about their respective habits. Rather than risking exposure, pathological gamblers and alcoholics become secretive and dishonest.

Frequent Disappearances

Both alcoholics and pathological gamblers spend a great deal of time fueling their disorders. As a result, they are often late for work, spend evenings away from home, take extended lunch breaks, or otherwise disappear for hours, or in some cases, days at a time. Alcoholics start drinking, usually with the intent of having a few drinks, but they rapidly become caught up with their consumption and lose control. The result is a bender that may last hours, or even days, during which the person may not come home, miss work, and so on. A similar process occurs with pathological gamblers. The individual begins gambling, with a limit in mind. However, the need to gamble usually overrides good intentions and subsequently results in a protracted gambling bender.

Although many of these behaviors are characteristic of problem drinkers and relief-and-escape gamblers, as well as alcoholics and pathological gamblers, the differentiating factors are the extensive and progressive deterioration and the loss of control, which are characteristic of the latter disorders, not the former.

Despite the similarities between the indicators of alcoholism and many of the indicators of pathological gambling, there are some signs that are unique to gambling.

Aberrant Behavior in Response to Sporting Events

Sports enthusiasts generally are happy if their favorite teams or athletes win and unhappy if they lose. However, when the event is over, such enthusiasts carry on with their lives. This scenario does not apply to pathological gamblers who bet on sports. Because these individuals are obsessed with winning, and because they bet heavily, the outcome of the event is both crucial and personalized. Pathological gamblers feel that their personal integrity is on the line. Thus, the pathological gambler's reaction to wins and losses appears exaggerated and extreme. If an individual consistently overreacts to the outcome of sporting events, this may be indicative of heavy gambling.

Excessive and Secretive Use of the Telephone

Many pathological gamblers rely upon the telephone to place their bets, especially those who bet on sporting events. Excessive and secretive use of the telephone is especially significant, if it occurs before and after games. On its own, however, excessive use of the telephone is fairly innocuous. It is only significant if it appears in concert with the other indicators previously described.

8
Probable Causes of Alcoholism and Pathological Gambling

Many individuals consume alcohol, and many gamble. However, despite the universal popularity of both activities, only a small percentage of the population develop problems with either or both. Of those who have problems with drinking or gambling, not all become dependent. This chapter looks at the possible reasons why some people become dependent upon one or the other.

Both alcoholism and pathological gambling are complex disorders, and no single theory to adequately explain how each develops has risen from the research. Indications are that each disorder develops from a complex interplay of biological, psychological, and sociological factors.

Biological Factors

Beginning with alcoholism, the assumption is that the disorder originates from a biological abnormality. It is thought that alterations in the physiological and biochemical functions of the body may render some people more susceptible than others to the effects of alcohol. What follows is a brief summary of some common biological theories.

One theory suggests that alcoholism may be a product of a malfunctioning endocrine system. This system consists of glands that secrete hormones and influence a variety of areas, including growth, sexual development, aspects of personality development, and resistance to disease. Although many pathological conditions are associated with a malfunctioning endocrine system, for people who are alcoholic and who also experience endocrinological problems, it is difficult to accurately determine if alcoholism is a result or a cause. Also, most alcoholics show no evidence of endocrine-system malfunction. Another theory suggests that alcoholism may be a form of food addiction. It is postulated that people who are alcoholic respond differently than others to the (food) by-products in alcohol beverages. So far, the most plausible biological explanation for the development of alcoholism is the possibility of genetic susceptibility.

It is frequently observed that alcoholism runs in families (American Psychiatric Association 1994; Fishman 1992). It has been noted that the risk of alcoholism is higher than average among close relatives of alcoholics, and that the coincidence of alcoholism is higher among monozygotic twins, than dyzygotic twins (American Psychiatric Association 1994). Further, studies reveal that the children of alcoholics who are taken at birth and adopted by families where there is no alcoholism, remain at high risk for developing the disorder (Fishman 1992). Fishman reports that the offspring of alcoholic parents, even if they are removed from their parents within a few weeks after birth, are more than three times likely to develop alcoholism than are children of non-alcoholic parents who are taken away just after birth.

The most widely held view of the relation between genetics and alcoholism, is that certain individuals may be born with a genetic predisposition to developing the disorder. In other words, they may be more susceptible to certain triggers, environmental or otherwise, that may produce alcoholism. A variety of biological abnormalities may be inherited and may lead to alcoholism. For example, some researchers postulate that alcoholism is the result of a biological imbalance in the body, which is moderated by drinking (Fishman 1992). Others believe that the alcoholic does not metabolize alcohol in a normal manner (Fishman 1992). Regardless, the biological theories do not explain how many children of alcoholics do not become alcoholics themselves and how the children of some nonalcoholics do.

Like some researchers of alcoholism, there are researchers who believe that pathological gambling is a product of deficiencies in biological functioning. For example, Rugle (1993) suggests that pathological gamblers may have both physiological and intrapsychic deficiencies, that subsequently impair the person's ability to learn from experience. Rugle claims that neuropsychological deficits impair pathological gamblers in their abilities to understand complex situations and to respond accordingly. This in turn interferes with the individual's ability to establish long-term goals, to accept delayed gratification, and to accurately anticipate consequences. Jacobs (1989) believes that pathological gamblers suffer from a state of chronic over or under arousal, and that gambling functions to stabilize them.

Research on pathological gambling also indicates the possibility of a genetic influence. Rosenthal (1992) cites evidence that indicates that between 18 percent and 43 percent of pathological gamblers have parents who abused alcohol or other drugs, and that between 20 percent and 28 percent had parents who had problems with gambling. Custer and Milt (1985) report that the children of compulsive gamblers (these authors use the term *compulsive* when referring to pathological gamblers) have a higher incidence than average of getting into trouble as teen-agers and of abusing drugs. Other research indicates that the children of pathological gamblers have a higher incidence of problems with drugs and a higher chance of developing eating disorders (Jacobs 1988). Ladouceur and Mireault (1988) found that high school students who had gambling problems were more likely to have parents who gambled heavily, than were students who did not have gambling problems. Henry (1996) theorizes that pathological gambling is a learned defense against anxiety and suggests that genetic variables, along with a history of trauma, may interplay to render some people more susceptible to losing control over gambling.

This evidence seems to indicate that, if genetic influences are a factor, the predisposition is not necessarily linear. In other words, the children of heavy gamblers appear to have a higher incidence of developing a multitude of problems that are not solely restricted to gambling. For example, studies suggest that the children of alcohol abusers, have a higher than average chance of becoming pathological gamblers. Interestingly, research on cocaine follows a similar pattern in that approximately 80 percent of cocaine addicts come from alcoholic families (Shulman 1987). These apparent inconsistencies may be explained by Jacob's (1988) research. He found that common dissociative states occur with both alcoholics and pathological gamblers. Jacob's research suggests that the common factor for any addictive disorder is a need to divorce oneself from reality, and that the method is a matter of personal choice whether it be gambling, alcohol, or drug consumption, or perhaps an eating disorder. Regardless of the evidence suggesting a biological underpinning for alcoholism and pathological gambling, genetic and other biological factors only explain part of the picture. Psychological and environmental factors also play important roles.

Psychological Factors

The psychological model suggests that psychological factors form the basis for the development of alcoholism and pathological gambling. With reference to alcoholism in particular, for many years professionals in the field believed that alcoholics had a distinct personality disorder, and that this disorder resulted in drinking to excess. However, most experts in the field of alcoholism research and treatment no longer endorse this theory (Fishman 1992). Although many alcoholics appear to share some common premorbid personality traits, such as low tolerance for frustration, low self-esteem, poor sexual identity, and feelings of isolation, it is difficult to determine if these are causal. Also, many people who develop alcoholism do not show evidence of having had these traits, and, conversely, many individuals who have these personality traits are not alcoholic.

With regard to pathological gambling, the evidence for and against a premorbid personality is equally equivocal. For example, Miller (1986) believes that pathological gamblers have feelings of inadequacy, and that gambling temporarily resolves these feelings. Glen (1979) believes that pathological gambling evolves in individuals who have deficits in abilities to plan, organize, and anticipate consequences. This in turn contributes to the pathological gambler's low tolerance for frustration and inability to learn from experience. However, as with alcoholism, it is difficult to determine if these personality attributes are causal or are a product of excessive gambling.

Psychoanalytic theories suggest that alcoholism or pathological gambling develops from unresolved psychological conflict that occurs in childhood. It is believed that alcohol consumption and gambling are coping devices to deal with the anxiety arising from these conflicts. Such theories advocate that alcoholism and pathological gambling are merely symptomatic of an underlying conflict, and that treatment should focus upon conflict resolution. However, experts agree that treatment intervention must also focus upon the behaviors of drinking and gambling and teach individuals healthy ways to relieve stress without gambling or drinking.

Other researchers claim that drinking or gambling is a learned behavior that is strengthened by stress reduction and the generation of pleasurable feelings. For example, the Social Learning Theory (Bandura 1969) advocates that the development of alcoholism is a product of a combination of pleasant pharmacological or drug-induced effects and social reinforcement variables. In the case of gambling, social reinforcement variables are considered solely influential. The Social Learning Theory postulates that many people begin drinking or gambling in a social manner, and that particular individuals use gambling or drinking to reduce stress, or to generate pleasurable feelings. Social variables like modeling influences, peer pressure, and cultural norms affect how people use alcohol or how they gamble. In other words, if an individual's environment encourages heavy drinking or gambling, if the individual enjoys the pleasurable effects of gambling or drinking, or if either activity is effective in reducing stress, then the individual is susceptible to developing alcoholism or pathological gambling.

The Social Learning Theory holds important implications for treatment. This theory predicts that if alcoholism and pathological gambling are learned behaviors, then they can be unlearned. This suggests that alcoholics and pathological gamblers should be able to learn how to moderate their drinking or their gambling behavior.

In the same manner that the biological theories do not fully endorse psychological and social influences, Social Learning Theory appears to minimize physiological variables, most specifically in relation to physical addiction. According to Fishman (1992), only about 5 to 10 percent of alcoholics are able to permanently moderate their alcohol consumption. This suggests that the abstinence model for the treatment of alcoholism should not be ignored. In the case of pathological gambling, abstinence may also be a viable route. To encourage moderation to the pathological gambler is to expose the individual to environmental influences that encourage heavy gambling.

Sociological Factors

The sociological model suggests that social and cultural factors play a major role in the development of both pathological gambling and alcoholism. Sociological variables include the incidence of alcohol consumption and gambling, societal attitudes toward either activity, social controls, affordability, and availability.

The level of alcohol consumption in a society appears to directly influence the incidence of alcoholism. The higher the *per capita* consumption, the greater the number of alcoholics (Core Knowledge in the Drug Field 1978). The incidence of alcoholism appears to be higher among cultures in which alcohol consumption is high, and lower among cultures with low levels of alcohol consumption. The same holds true with gambling. The amount of drinking or gambling in a society also impacts upon societal attitudes, which in turn influence how much people drink or gamble. If societal attitudes are positive, then consumption is higher.

Social controls influence how much drinking and gambling occurs. Typically, the incidence of alcoholism and pathological gambling is higher in societies that exert few legal and social controls over alcohol consumption and gambling. For example, during the early days of prohibition in Canada, the incidence of alcoholism decreased correspondingly with the decrease in the general level of consumption (Core Knowledge in the Drug Field 1978). The levels of both drinking and gambling are also influenced by affordability and availability. It is more difficult to drink or to gamble, if limited by accessibility or affordability.

Holistic Approach

Fishman (1992) describes a holistic approach to explain alcoholism. This approach may also apply to pathological gambling. His view suggests that the development of either disorder is influenced by environmental variables, while acknowledging that some individuals are more psychologically vulnerable and others more genetically predisposed to the development of either alcoholism or pathological gambling. The holistic approach also takes into account that, at least in the case of alcoholism, both a physical and a psychological addiction are usually present.

Types of Alcoholics and Pathological Gamblers

There appears to be more than one type of alcoholic. In my book (1989), I define primary alcoholics as individuals who show indications of alcoholism from when they first begin drinking. The most probable explanation for this type of alcoholic is a genetic or inherited susceptibility.

By contrast, secondary alcoholics are individuals who do not start out being alcoholic. Rather, they begin drinking in response to some long-term underlying physical or emotional problem. Alcohol is consumed as a method of blunting discomfort, such as chronic pain, anxiety, depression, insomnia, etc. With time, the prolonged consumption of alcohol leads to a dependence.

Some individuals are reactive alcoholics. They drink heavily in response to an acute stressor, such as a death of someone close, a marriage break-up, or a job loss. They drink to forget their problems, and sometimes an addiction develops.

The fourth type of alcoholic is someone who starts out as a social drinker. Because the person likes either the taste or the effects of alcohol, he or she chooses to drink increasingly greater amounts, or drink more frequently. Regardless, as drinking is pursued, alcoholism insidiously develops.

When looking at the development of pathological gambling, similar patterns emerge. Regardless of why they start gambling, some people show signs of pathological gambling from the very beginning. Again, this suggests a genetic predisposition. Others start gambling to escape from problems, which results in a dependence for some. Still others begin as social gamblers, enjoy the game and gamble more frequently. For some, social gambling gradually gives way to pathological gambling.

9

Psychological Factors that Sustain Pathological Gambling and Alcoholism

This chapter deals with psychological processes that contribute to the development of pathological gambling and of alcoholism. Because the characteristics of pathological gambling and alcoholism are so similar, with a few exceptions, the psychological factors that contribute to the development of pathological gambling and function to sustain the disorder are also relevant for alcoholism.

Pathological gamblers believe that they cannot function without gambling. They are preoccupied with thoughts of gambling, and when they are not gambling, they feel as if something is missing. The same applies to alcoholics and their alcohol. Even if some pathological gamblers or alcoholics engage in their respective habits on an episodic basis, thoughts of doing so linger in the background. This chapter looks at specific psychological factors which perpetuate gambling and drinking behaviors.

Operant Conditioning

Operant conditioning (sometimes referred to as instrumental conditioning) is a powerful type of learning that occurs when a response is made to a stimulus and a reinforcement follows. The result is that the same response to the stimulus becomes more likely in the future. Consequently, in operant conditioning, a reinforcer is anything that strengthens the probability of occurrence of a response to a stimulus. For example, if a person watches (a response) a particular television show (a stimulus) for the first time and really enjoys it (a reinforcement), this increases the chance of the person watching the show again. If each episode is enjoyable, this further strengthens the individual's watching behavior. In other words, the behavior of watching that particular show is reinforced, thereby increasing the chance of that behavior occurring again.

There are two types of reinforcers. One type, a primary reinforcer, functions to satisfy a basic need, such as hunger, thirst, a need for pleasure, sexual relief, and so on. Primary reinforcers are also those that reduce discomfort. Another type, a secondary reinforcer, is anything that through association with a primary reinforcer acquires properties that are either identical or similar to the primary reinforcer. One of the most powerful secondary reinforcers is money. The paper from which our legal tender is made is basically valueless. However, because money can buy many primary and secondary reinforcers, people will work hard (i.e., become operantly conditioned) to acquire that paper.

Both primary and secondary reinforcers may be further divided into positive and negative reinforcers. A positive reinforcer is something that is pleasant or desirable.

Consequently, positive reinforcement involves following a response with something that is pleasant or desirable. By contrast, negative reinforcement is the process of following a response with the reduction or elimination of something that is undesirable. This is the opposite of punishment, which involves following a response with something that is undesirable or aversive. Both positive and negative reinforcement function to strengthen behavior; the first introduces a positive consequence and the second reduces or eliminates something that causes discomfort. Punishment on the other hand, weakens behavior by introducing an aversive consequence. For example, a lady goes to a clothing store and tries on a new coat. She likes how the coat looks on her (positive reinforcement) and she also feels comfortable wearing it (positive reinforcement). Consequently, she purchases the coat. The lady wears the coat outside and does not feel cold (negative reinforcement). So far, the behavior of wearing the coat has been strengthened by how the coat looks, feels, and eliminates discomfort. After wearing the coat in the rain, the lady discovers that the coat does not look good when it is wet (punishment). Consequently, she decides to never wear it in the rain. The behavior of wearing the coat in the rain is weakened by a punishing consequence.

Factors which Influence Reinforcement

Three factors affect the efficacy of reinforcement. These are the delay, the amount, and the timing of reinforcement (Freedman 1978). The delay of reinforcement refers to how long it takes for a reinforcer to occur after a response is made. The greater the delay, the less effective the reinforcement. If the delay is too long, operant conditioning does not occur. For example, with reference to the lady and the coat, if the lady tries on the coat, but is told she would have to wait a long time before seeing herself in the mirror, she might leave the store without waiting or purchasing the coat.

The amount or size of reinforcement also affects behavior. If an individual behaves in a particular manner and the payoff is minimal, the probability of that behavior occurring again is less than if the reinforcement were substantial. For example, if an individual watches a television program and derives only minimal enjoyment (i.e., receives minimal reinforcement), there is little likelihood of the individual again watching the show.

The third factor that influences the effectiveness of reinforcement is the timing of occurrence. The timing of reinforcement is referred to as the schedule of reinforcement (Ruch and Zimbardo 1971). Schedules of reinforcement have a significant influence upon people in a variety of ways. For example, most students want to know how often tests will be scheduled and what mark is required to pass. This knowledge lets them know how much studying is required.

Whether they know it or not, people are greatly influenced by schedules of reinforcement. Factory workers who are paid according to how much they produce, tend to work harder than those on a fixed salary. A person's sleeping and eating behavior is usually affected by whether it is a work day or a vacation day (work days typically have different schedules of reinforcement than vacation days). Some of the schedules of reinforcement, like how often a person receives his or her paycheck, are obvious. Others, such as the influence of the weather, are more haphazard.

There are different types of schedules of reinforcement. Continuous reinforcement occurs when an individual receives a reinforcer every time the behavior occurs. An example is clicking the remote control and having the television come on. Another example is always getting a high mark for studying hard.

Intermittent reinforcement occurs when the behavior is reinforced only some of the time. For example, a boy asks a girl for a date on a regular basis, but she only accepts on some occasions. To confuse the issue even more, there are different types of intermittent reinforcement. A fixed-ratio schedule of reinforcement occurs when the same number of behaviors receives a reinforcement every time. For example, a weight trainer may require a student to always bench press eight repetitions before giving the person a rest (a reinforcement). A variable-ratio schedule occurs when a reinforcement comes after a variable and unpredictable number of responses are made. An example is playing hockey. A goal is not scored on every shot. Usually differing numbers of shots are required. A fixed-interval schedule of reinforcement occurs when the frequency of a reinforcement is not determined by the number of responses, as are the ratio schedules, but rather by a fixed passage of time. A classical example is an individual on salary. The person receives the same paycheck, although the amount of work, i.e., the number of responses that the individual makes, varies from paycheck to paycheck. The fourth type of schedule, the variable-interval schedule, results when reinforcers occur after varying periods of time. Watching a sporting event (where an exciting action or a goal is a reinforcement) is an example. The occurrence of reinforcement is not timed such that the intervals between reinforcements are the same. It should be noted that while the viewers of a sporting event are on a variable interval schedule of reinforcement, the players are on a variable ratio schedule.

Different schedules of reinforcement affect the rates of response, i.e., how fast and for how long people engage in various activities. Ratio schedules of reinforcement tend to produce very high rates of behavior, whereas interval schedules result in lower rates of response. For example, individuals performing piecework, receive reinforcement (money) according to how many responses they make (e.g., how many jeans they stitch). In the latter case, people get paid whether they work or not, whereas in the former, the individual only gets paid for working.

Analysis of Gambling Behavior

Gambling behavior involves both powerful primary and secondary reinforcement, and it also involves punishment. When people gamble, their (gambling) behavior is reinforced by occasionally winning money (secondary reinforcement). As a matter of fact, three-quarters of people entering treatment for pathological gambling, report that winning money is their main reason for gambling (Legg England, and Gotestam 1991). Typically, there are other reinforcers, such as the excitement of gambling (primary reinforcement), enjoying gambling with friends (primary reinforcement), and so on. Because the excitement produced by gambling is both rapid, and for some individuals very intense, gambling behavior meets all of the criteria for the quick occurrence of operant conditioning. There is negligible delay of reinforcement, and the amount of reinforcement is often significant. For those people who do not experience much pleasure from gambling, conditioning is much weaker, and for some it never occurs at all.

The difference between pathological gamblers and social gamblers, appears to be related to the level of excitement (primary reinforcement) which gambling produces.
Winning provides pathological gamblers with a sense of
euphoria, whereas social gamblers do not experience this
type of excitement. Although wanting to win money, pathological gamblers also gamble for the euphoric effects (Legg
England, and Gotestam 1991).

In addition to primary and secondary positive reinforcement, some individuals receive negative reinforcement
from gambling. Certain people gamble to relieve depression
and boredom, and for distraction from their worries. Legg
England, and Gotestam (1991) found that many pathological gamblers gamble to forget their troubles and to relieve
depression. Rather than gamble as a social activity and for
the excitement, many people gamble for escape (Specter,
Carlson, Edmonson, Johnson, and Marcotte 1996). Further,
these researchers found that avoidant gambling is more
common with women than with men. If an individual's
gambling results in financial, legal, or family difficulties
(i.e., punishment), then the negative reinforcement (escape
component) of gambling becomes even more significant.
Jacobs (1989) found that for pathological gamblers, gambling produces a dissociative state that satisfies a need for
escape.

Individuals who are able to control how much they
gamble usually avoid experiencing trouble. They are able to
stop their gambling before they lose too much money or before gambling interferes with family or other activities.
However, pathological gamblers find it difficult to control
their gambling. Many only stop when they run out of
money, or they are too exhausted to continue. They experience difficulties as a consequence of their gambling, feel

subsequent remorse and guilt, and pursue gambling for relief. Typically, pathological gamblers are caught in
binge/crash/craving cycles. They binge gamble to exhaustion, or until they have lost all of their available money.
This is followed by crash periods of intense remorse and
craving, which are relieved by further gambling. Pathological gamblers are trapped in a gambling cycle.

The Pathological Gambling Cycle

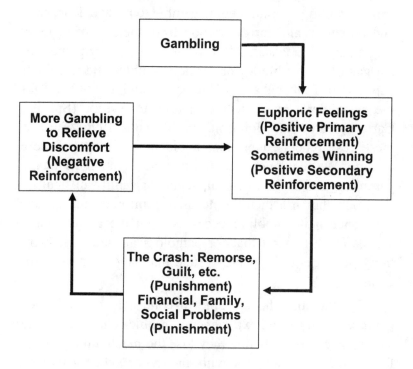

Once started, it is difficult for pathological gamblers
to extract themselves from this cycle. To do so they must be
willing to face and to deal with problems accumulated

through gambling, as well as to weather a host of uncomfortable feelings. However, because these problems appear monumental, the gambler experiences severe dysphoria. Because the gambler is so habituated to avoidance, abstinence seems unfathomable.

Besides the Pathological Gambling Cycle, gambling behavior is also acquired and maintained by schedules of reinforcement (Walters 1994). The winning component of gambling follows a variable ratio schedule of reinforcement. In other words, the number of responses required for a reinforcement (i.e., winning) is variable and, therefore, unpredictable. Consequently, pathological gamblers feel that a big win is always imminent. They are afraid to stop, especially when they are losing, because the next roll of dice, the next hand of cards, the next display on a slot machine, or the next race, may just result in the big win. This type of schedule is very resistant to extinction (Freedman 1978).

A win is a reinforcer, but so is a near miss. Reid (1986) found that almost winning (i.e., a failure that is close to being successful) acts as an intermediate reinforcer for the pathological gambler. Near misses appear to induce more gambling. They provide the gambler with renewed hope that a big win is imminent.

The fact that pathological gambling seems more likely to develop for certain forms of gambling, as opposed to others, suggests that reinforcement contingencies are influential. Types of gambling such as video lottery terminals, slot machines, horse racing, and casino games such as roulette, where the reinforcement is immediate, are more problematic than other types of gambling, such as lotteries, where the reinforcement is delayed (Legg England, and Gotestam 1991).

Analysis of Drinking Behavior

Alcoholics consume alcohol for reasons that are very similar to why pathological gamblers gamble. Alcoholics drink for two main reasons: to create pleasurable feelings and to eliminate discomfort. Like gambling, alcohol consumption produces sought-after effects that are immediate. Drinking results in immediate pleasure and the immediate reduction of discomfort. However, because alcoholics usually drink too much and at the wrong times, trouble occurs. To eliminate feelings of discomfort caused by the trouble, they drink even more. Like pathological gamblers, alcoholics become trapped in a cycle.

The Alcoholism Drinking Cycle, which I described in 1989, involves 1) the alcoholic drinking to acquire pleasurable feelings (positive reinforcement), 2) acting inappropriately while under the influence, 3) experiencing problems as a consequence, and subsequently feeling guilt, anxiety, and depression (punishment), and 4) drinking for relief from these feelings (negative reinforcement). Like the pathological gambler who attempts to quit gambling, an alcoholic who attempts to quit drinking must weather a host of uncomfortable emotions, and resolve a variety of problems caused by drinking.

Alcoholism Drinking Cycle

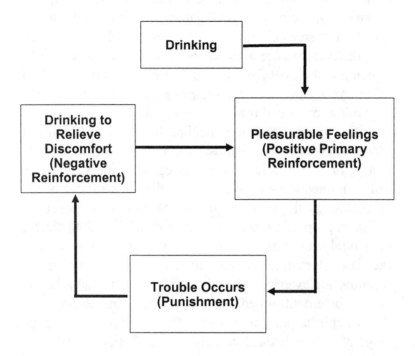

Besides drinking to ward off uncomfortable feelings arising from the trouble caused by drinking, many alcoholics often persist in drinking to avoid the unpleasant effects of alcohol withdrawal. Although pathological gamblers report restlessness and irritability when attempting to reduce or arrest their gambling (Rosenthal 1992), they do not experience the type of discomfort akin to the physical withdrawal from alcohol, which includes tremors, anxiety, restlessness, and in severe cases, delirium, hallucinations, and convulsive seizures.

While many alcoholics face a potentially serious detoxification reaction (which in some cases may be life-threatening), the pathological gambler does not (unless the gambler is also alcoholic or otherwise drug addicted). However, the pattern of reinforcement for pathological gamblers is such that their benders can last longer than those for alcoholics. As alcoholics drink, their immediate supply of alcohol and/or money diminishes proportionally. Also, if an alcoholic consumes enough alcohol, the individual will fall asleep or lose consciousness. Running out of alcohol or money, or falling asleep or losing consciousness, prevents further immediate consumption. In the case of gambling, the pathological gamblers' supply of money does not diminish in proportion to the extent of gambling. Sometimes, substantial wins provide gamblers with more money than when they started. Even intermittent small wins may sustain gambling for extensive periods. As a matter of fact, the ratio reinforcement schedules for winning in casinos and other establishments, are set up in such a way to keep people gambling for extensive periods. In contrast, alcoholics do not create money with which to purchase more alcohol while they drink.

When it comes to drinking, alcoholics are on a continuous reinforcement schedule. Every time an alcoholic consumes alcohol, the individual is reinforced with pleasurable feelings, as well as the reduction or the elimination of uncomfortable ones. The pathological gambler, on the other hand, is influenced by two schedules of reinforcement. One is a continuous reinforcement schedule on which the reinforcement of pleasure and the reduction or elimination of discomfort occurs each time the person gambles. The other is a ratio schedule of reinforcement, related specifically to winning.

Classical Conditioning

Classical conditioning occurs when a stimulus that initially does not produce a response comes to acquire the ability to produce a response by pairing it with a stimulus that produces the response. An unconditioned stimulus is one that automatically produces a response, referred to as an unconditioned response, and the neutral stimulus that comes to produce the response by being paired with an unconditioned stimulus is referred to as a conditioned stimulus. The response produced by the conditioned stimulus is called a conditioned response. The following diagram clarifies the process.

Classical Conditioning Paradigm

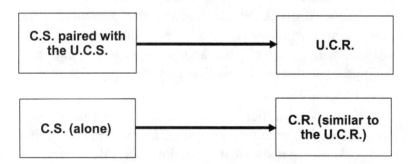

The unconditioned stimulus (U.C.S.) is one that, without any learning, produces an unconditioned response (U.C.R.). The conditioned stimulus (C.S.) is one that, by being paired with the U.C.S., acquires the ability to produce a conditioned response (C.R.). The conditioned response is usually similar, and sometimes identical, to the unconditioned response. For example, the mere sight of a restaurant building may elicit salivation in a hungry person. By being paired with food (an unconditioned stimulus), the building has become a conditioned stimulus.

The strength of classical conditioning is a function of the interval between the occurrence of the neutral stimulus and the occurrence of the unconditioned stimulus. The neutral stimulus must occur just prior to the occurrence of the unconditioned stimulus for conditioning to occur. If the delay between the occurrence of the neutral stimulus and the unconditioned stimulus is too long, there is no association and classical conditioning does not occur.

Wikler (1948) first recognized the role of classical conditioning in drug addiction. He found that heroin and morphine addicts who are in recovery experience cravings and feelings of withdrawal, whenever they talk about the drugs or whenever they are exposed to situations in which they had used drugs. Wikler refers to this phenomenon as "conditioned withdrawal." He believes that these environmental stimuli acquired the ability to elicit cravings and feelings of withdrawal, and that they play a major role in triggering relapses.

Classical conditioning plays an important role in alcoholism and, in the author's opinion, an even more significant role in pathological gambling. Besides being a powerful primary reinforcer, alcohol is also a powerful unconditioned stimulus. When alcohol is consumed, it elicits a reaction in the body, i.e., an unconditioned response. Other stimuli that are paired with alcohol consumption will through association come to elicit conditioned responses similar to that produced by alcohol. For example, the sight of a bar, drinking buddies, certain foods, particular times of the day, and so on, may elicit pleasurable feelings and cravings to drink.

A similar process occurs with gambling. For the pathological gambler, the act of gambling is an unconditioned stimulus. It produces unconditioned responses such as excitement and the elimination of dysphoria. Here, too, a vast array of stimuli, such as gambling establishments, slot machines, race tracks, horses, cards, sporting events, and so on, acquire conditioned properties that may elicit cravings to gamble.

However, classical conditioning may be more powerful for the pathological gambler than for the alcoholic. As alcoholics become progressively more intoxicated, they become less aware of their environment (Fishman 1992). In other words, the reduction in an intoxicated individual's sensitivity to environmental stimuli reduces the chance of classical conditioning. If a person is too drunk to notice the surroundings, associations with environmental stimuli are less likely to occur. In the case of pathological gamblers, the excitement of gambling may temporarily increase environmental awareness, thus allowing for strong associations and, therefore, classical conditioning to occur. These environmental stimulus cues create powerful urges to gamble. Cummings, Gordon, and Marlatt (1980) found that environmental stimulus cues are very influential in triggering relapses in pathological gamblers.

It is important to recognize that environmental stimulus cues may be associated with a gambling-positive effect, such as the excitement of gambling, winning money, euphoria, the relief of uncomfortable emotions, the feeling of escape and so on. Other environmental stimulus cues may be associated with a gambling-negative effect, such as losing money and the feelings associated with it, such as anxiety, panic, and depression. In other words, some stimuli in the pathological gambler's environment, through association with the positives of gambling, produce pleasant emotions, and, alternatively, some stimuli, through association with the negatives of gambling, produce uncomfortable emotions. Some stimuli may even have a competing effect, thus producing concurrent positive and negative responses.

The need of pathological gamblers to increase the size of their bets may be explained by the presence of both positive and negative environmental stimulus cues. If pathological gamblers find that gambling makes them feel both good and bad at the same time, they may inadvertently find themselves betting greater amounts, or betting more frequently, in order to create excitement or a reduction of discomfort that rises above the competing conditioned responses from the positive and negative environmental stimulus cues. Because alcoholics become too intoxicated to be sensitive to environmental stimuli, their need to consume increasingly greater quantities of alcohol is usually fueled by physical tolerance.

Besides freeing themselves from the Pathological Gambling Cycle, pathological gamblers in recovery must, at least for the short-term, avoid as many environmental stimulus cues as possible. Failure to do so usually results in cue-induced cravings to gamble. After awhile, if a conditioned stimulus is not associated with the unconditioned stimulus, the conditioned stimulus loses its potency to elicit a conditioned response. This is referred to as extinction. If the pathological gambler stops gambling and remains abstinent, the conditioned stimuli associated with gambling eventually lose their potency. Alcoholics in recovery must also avoid environmental stimuli, such as bars and other situations, in which drinking is expected.

Spontaneous Recovery in Classical Conditioning

When a conditioned stimulus is repeatedly presented in the absence of the unconditioned stimulus, the association between the two eventually weakens and disappears. In other words, the previously conditioned stimulus loses its ability to elicit a conditioned response. However, if there is a rest period during which the previously conditioned stimulus is not presented, and if it is then presented, conditioning may spontaneously re-occur where a conditioned response is elicited. For example, the bells that ring in a casino when a individual has a big win, may become conditioned stimuli for a pathological gambler, such that even when the individual is not at a casino but happens to hear a bell, a craving to gamble is elicited. If this person stops gambling, eventually the sound of a bell will lose its potency. However, if the person does not hear a bell for an extensive period and then hears one, cravings to gamble may occur. In other words, even after months of abstinence from gambling, a stimulus that had previously lost its ability to produce cravings, may elicit a craving. Caught off guard, some individuals feel overwhelmed by sudden cravings and relapse. Although alcoholics are also susceptible to the phenomenon of spontaneous recovery, it is not as strong for them because classical conditioning does not appear to be as strong.

Contiguity Association

Contiguity association is a type of learning that occurs when two seemingly unrelated stimuli, appear together by chance and become linked in a individual's memory. Later, if the person is exposed to one of the stimuli, the other comes to mind. This type of learning is very basic, fast, and often occurs unnoticed. Unlike either operant conditioning or classical conditioning, this type of learning is spontaneous and unpredictable. Consequently, it may produce "surprise" environmental stimulus cues for the addicted person. For no apparent reason, the pathological gambler or the alcoholic may experience sudden cravings in the presence of a particular stimulus.

Learning Interactions

The various types of learning do not occur in isolation. They interact to accentuate the pleasurable effects of either gambling or drinking, as well as to produce powerful cravings for further use. For example, the thought of gambling or the sight or sound of any stimuli associated with gambling, may create powerful cravings for the pathological gambler. Depending upon whether the cues are positive or negative, the gambler may experience excitement or discomfort in response to these stimuli. Either feeling, or a combination of both, creates a need to gamble. The same applies to the alcoholic and drinking. If the pathological gambler does gamble, the action will be negatively reinforced through craving reduction, and positively reinforced through feeling pleasure or excitement. Again, the same applies to the alcoholic and drinking. As these individuals partake in their respective habits, more neutral stimuli, either through classical conditioning or contiguity association, become conditioned stimuli, thus eliciting conditioned responses that are relieved only by more drinking, or gambling. Typically, trouble occurs, making more gambling or drinking, necessary for relief. This enmeshment of learning variables and their effects makes both alcoholism and pathological gambling very resistant to treatment.

10
Physical Factors That Sustain Alcoholism and Pathological Gambling

Physical dependence to alcohol is manifested by tolerance and a withdrawal reaction when an individual stops drinking. Tolerance is evidenced where an individual requires increased amounts of alcohol to produce an effect. Alcohol withdrawal or detoxification is characterized by anxiety, restlessness, diaphoresis, hypertension, rapid pulse, and delirium and convulsive seizures in severe cases.

From a physiological perspective, alcohol consumption depresses or slows down the functioning of the brain and other organs. The amount of alcohol-induced depression is partially a function of how fast an individual drinks. For most healthy adults, consuming one drink per hour will not lead to significant intoxication. In other words, one drink per hour allows the liver to metabolize the alcohol at a rate approximately equal to how fast it is taken into the body. If a person consumes alcohol faster than the body breaks it down, intoxication occurs. Because alcoholics usually drink large amounts fairly quickly, they consume alcohol faster than their bodies are able to eliminate it. Consequently they become drunk. However, how fast an individual drinks is not an isolated variable. The effect of alcohol also depends upon body size. Larger people have a higher blood volume, and, therefore, an equal amount of alcohol will generally have less effect upon a larger individual than upon a smaller person. The same amount of alcohol will be more concentrated in the lower blood volume of a smaller person. Additionally, having food in one's stomach slows down the rate of alcohol absorption, and the subsequent intoxication.

The first part of the brain that is affected by alcohol ingestion is the outer layer, the cerebral cortex (Fishman 1992). This area of the brain controls speech, judgment, ability to sense stimuli, and ability to accurately perceive one's environment. In other words, as an individual becomes progressively intoxicated on alcohol, speech becomes slurred, logical thinking and judgment are impaired, and the person becomes less perceptive of the environment.

Emotional changes include a sense of well-being, a state of reverie, and diminished emotional inhibition. Alcoholics find these feelings pleasurable.

Continued drinking affects the cerebellum (Fishman 1992), which is the posterior area of the brain and controls balance and physical coordination. Impairment of this region of the brain results in a staggering gait, lack of motor coordination, and falls. The next area of the brain to be affected is the limbic system, which mediates memory and control of one's emotions. This is why alcohol intoxication often causes memory lapses and emotional extremes including loud speech, aggressiveness, withdrawal, exaggerated laughter, physical violence, and so on.

Even though alcohol is a depressant, it occasionally appears to act as a stimulant. This is due to alcohol depressing those parts of the brain which control emotions and judgment, and is a major reason why alcoholics often experience trouble. When intoxicated, alcoholics lose control of their emotions. In combination with impaired judgment, this leads to inappropriate behavior. Consequently, alcoholics are faced with a perpetual dilemma. They enjoy diminished emotional inhibition, but they do not enjoy the trouble that frequently follows. The alcoholic resolves this dilemma through a type of twisted thinking referred to as denial. This type of thinking allows the alcoholic to really believe that the trouble is not a result of drinking. This unhealthy process of distorting reality is dealt with in more detail in the next chapter.

Some individuals consume very large amounts of alcohol, and their brain function becomes so depressed that they lose consciousness. In extreme cases, a person may become comatose. This may be life-threatening, because large doses of alcohol inhibit respiration (breathing), and may result in cardiac arrest. The effects of alcohol follow the typical stages of anesthesia described by Lee (1959). The first stage consists of a depression of the sensory cortex. The second stage results in a loss of self-control over emotions and, depending upon the emotional state of the person, exaggerated reactions including violence may occur. The third stage results in respiratory paralysis, and the fourth produces cardiac failure and death.

Because alcoholics are trapped in the Alcoholism Drinking Cycle (Chapter 9), many feel compelled to continue drinking. To stop drinking results in the discomfort of withdrawal, as well as a host of uncomfortable feelings related to the troubles caused by drinking. Alcoholics drink because they believe that it is the only way to feel good. This results in a pattern of chronic drinking.

Effects of Chronic Drinking

Regardless of the pleasure or the emotional relief that alcohol consumption produces, heavy drinking is not without serious physical consequences. Alcohol is distributed by the blood to all areas of the body. Because alcohol is toxic, the body attempts to defend itself against the drug. One way that the body protects itself against heavy alcohol intake, is to metabolize alcohol more quickly. This results in the liver working harder and more efficiently (Fishman 1992). The second way the body compensates for heavy drinking is to adapt. During adaptation, the cells of the body increase their speed of performance to counteract the depressing effects of alcohol (Fishman 1992). In other words, the liver works harder and more efficiently, and the cells of the body work faster, which results the individual becoming less sensitive to the effects of alcohol. This is referred to as tolerance. As the tolerance level increases, alcoholics must increase their alcohol consumption to realize an effect. In turn, this forces the body to work even harder. Whenever an alcoholic stops drinking, the depressing effects of alcohol wear off, but usually the body is still in a speeded-up mode. The effect is anxiety, restlessness, and, in extreme cases, hallucinations and convulsive seizures. Because alcohol withdrawal is so uncomfortable, the person drinks to avoid it.

The body cannot maintain its defense against heavy drinking indefinitely. Eventually, cells and organs begin to break down. Fishman (1992) describes a variety of physical consequences of this breakdown process, including swollen and inflamed organs, such as inflammation of the heart (myocarditis), stomach (gastritis), liver (hepatitis), pancreas (pancreatitis), and the nerves (neuritis). Cirrhosis (destruction of liver cells), which usually follows hepatitis, is potentially life threatening. Like other organs, the brain is also adversely affected. Many chronic alcoholics show evidence of brain damage, indicated by significant deficits in recent memory, concentration, logic, comprehension, and abstract reasoning.

Pathological Gambling

Unlike alcoholism, pathological gambling does not involve the ingestion of a toxic substance. However, there is evidence that pathological gambling does have physical implications, which function to perpetuate the disorder. As mentioned, the limbic system is believed to control emotions and consummatory behavior, such as eating (Freedman 1978). This system includes the hypothalamus, hippocampus, septum, and amygdala. In many animals, including primates, experimental manipulation of parts of the limbic system evokes emotions (Freedman 1978). Some areas of the limbic system also appear to play a role in memory and to operate as reward centers. In other words, feelings of pleasure appear to generate from this area. Because many pathological gamblers describe feelings of euphoria when gambling, this suggests that gambling behavior may somehow impact upon the reward centers of the brain. For some gamblers, the sense of pleasure generated by gambling is so intense, that it resembles the euphoria of the cocaine high (Rosenthal, 1992) or that produced by amphetamines or opiates (Legg England, and Gotestam 1991).

There are chemicals in the brain, referred to as neuro-transmitters, that are believed to influence body functioning. Three particular neurotransmitters are significant, with reference to the effects of cocaine. These are dopamine, norepinephrine, and serotonin (Landry and Smith 1987). Ingestion of cocaine is thought to temporarily increase the level of dopamine in the brain, thus producing the cocaine high (Herridge and Gold 1988; Dakis and Gold 1985). Cocaine binds with dopamine-transporter proteins that are really supposed to bind with dopamine released from the neurons, and subsequently carry the dopamine back to the neurons. This recycling process is referred to as reuptake. However, by binding with the proteins, cocaine prevents reuptake by blocking dopamine from being taken back into the neurons, thus causing a build up of dopamine and the subsequent cocaine high. Landry and Smith (1987) believe that cocaine has its greatest effect upon the limbic system. Because the pleasurable effect of cocaine is so powerful, it overrides any desire for food, water, sleep, and often sex (Herscovitch 1995). Cocaine addicts go on cocaine benders, that usually end only when the individual runs out of cocaine or is exhausted. The gambling benders of many pathological gamblers parallel that of cocaine addicts. These gamblers usually quit gambling only when they are exhausted or run out of money. In my book (1995), I discuss how cocaine use also alters levels of norepinephrine, resulting in tachycardia (accelerated heart rate) and hypertension (high blood pressure), and the levels of serotonin, resulting in insomnia. Many pathological gamblers are also plagued with insomnia.

Because pathological gamblers have feelings and behaviors similar to cocaine addicts and other drug addicts, it is conceivable that gambling may impact upon neurotrans-

mitter levels, thus producing effects similar to those of cocaine and other drugs. Some research indicates that pathological gamblers may have an abnormality in their
noradrenergic system (Roy, Adinoff, Roehrich, Custer, Lorenz, and Linnoila 1988). In research tests, pathological
gamblers were found to have higher levels of urinary output
of norepinephrine than the control subjects. Epstein (1989)
talks about how gambling may increase dopamine levels in
the brain. Other researchers believe that many activities, including gambling, alter brain neurotransmitter activity just
as chemicals do (Hyman 1994; Hyman and Nestler 1993;
Milkman and Sunderwirth 1987). Wickelgren (1997) is of
the opinion that dopamine may play more than a direct role
as most of the research suggests. Wickelgren presents some
very preliminary research, which suggests that dopamine
releases in the brain are believed not only to produce pleasure, but also draw attention to events (stimuli) that predict
rewards. In other words, dopamine may be an aid to learning. Nesse and Berridge (1997) take the case a bit further.
They differentiate between "wanting" and "liking," within
the context of addiction. They refer to "liking" as the "he-
donic pleasure of receiving a reward," and "wanting" as
"incentive motivation and behavioral pursuit of a reward."
According to these authors, liking (effects of the receipt of
a reward) is mediated by opioid forebrain systems. Wanting
is based upon learned expectations and may result in compulsive drug-seeking behavior. Given that pathological
gambling behaviors run parallel, this process may be applicable to gambling as well. If this research and subsequent
speculation turns out to be accurate, it indicates a physiological underlay for the operant and classical conditioning
processes of pathological gambling and alcoholism. In other
words, it is possible that pathological gambling is not

merely driven by psychological phenomena, but also by physical phenomena.

Further evidence exists for a physiological basis to gambling disorders. For example, researchers have found that excessive gambling produces significant changes in heart rate (Dickerson 1989). Anderson and Brown (1984) found that gambling produced significant increases in heart rate. Going a step further, Griffiths (1993) found that while gambling, regular and occasional gamblers showed no significant differences in increase in heart rate, but after gambling, the heart rate of regular gamblers decreased rapidly but this did not occur for occasional gamblers. It is surmised that pathological gamblers play frequently and for higher stakes as a way of maintaining physiological arousal, as indicated by increased heart rate. Because occasional gamblers appear to stay aroused for longer periods after gambling, compared to regular gamblers, this may by why occasional gamblers do not feel compelled to gamble for as long or as frequently. Griffiths believes that regular gamblers develop tolerance to the arousal of gambling. Hence, they have to gamble more quickly and more frequently.

It appears that some form of physiological arousal is a major reinforcer for heavy gamblers, and that this excitement is probably autonomic (mediated by that part of the nervous system that produces feelings of excitement) and/or cortical (Brown 1987). Griffiths (1993, p. 366) states "it appears that sociological variables may account for the acquisition of gambling behavior, whereas physiological and psychological variables may be particularly important in maintenance." Legg England, and Gotestam (1991, p. 115) state; "There is considerable evidence that gambling represents a significant physiological, emotional and mental event for those who gamble excessively."

Many gambling establishments are well lit and noisy. Winners are acclaimed by ringing bells, shouts of "bingo," and so on. Griffiths (1990) found that a significant number of gamblers reported that the visual and auditory stimulation was an important factor in maintaining their gambling behavior. He also found that pathological gamblers appear to be more attracted to this stimulation than non-pathological gamblers.

Jacobs (1989) suggests that pathological gamblers may have a physiological predisposition toward chronic states of either hyperarousal or hypoarousal. He believes that for the pathological gambler, the act of gambling functions to bring physiological arousal to comfortable levels by increasing arousal for some and decreasing arousal for others. The type of gambling that pathological gamblers choose functions to alter arousal levels accordingly. Jacobs goes on to say that over or under arousal is a physiological precondition that renders an individual susceptible to the development of pathological gambling, and that environmental variables further provoke this development. He believes that people with strong feelings of inferiority, inadequacy, low self-esteem, and a sense of rejection, and who also experience chronic over or under arousal, are more susceptible to the development of any addiction, including pathological gambling. This theory is supported by evidence that negative relationships are often observed in the family backgrounds of pathological gamblers (Lesieur, Blume, and Zoppa 1986).

Clinicians in the field of chemical dependency have noted that some people enjoy the sedating and relaxing effects of alcohol, and conversely, they do not like the arousal effects of cocaine. The reverse is true for still others. For these individuals, their choice of drug may be predetermined by their arousal levels. For pathological gamblers, the choice of particular types of gambling may function similarly. Custer and Milt (1985) describe two types of pathological gamblers: those who gamble for excitement, and others who gamble for escape. In other words, certain forms of gambling may allow individuals to distract themselves from their worries, i.e., escape, thereby reducing their levels of arousal, and others gamble for excitement, thereby increasing their levels of arousal.

Some EEG studies show irregularities in the brain activity of pathological gamblers. Carlton and Manowitz (1994) found that the EEG characteristics of pathological gamblers paralleled those seen in children with Attention Deficit Disorder. It may be that the gambling behavior of some pathological gamblers is a form of compensation for deficits in brain functioning.

Studies on the effects of exercise may also be relevant to the understanding of pathological gambling. For example, regular exercise appears to amplify the effects of certain brain chemicals called endogenous opiates (endorphins, enkephalins, dynorphins) (Smith 1986). These chemicals appear to be linked to a sense of well-being. It may be that for certain people, intense gambling functions similarly to exercise, thus causing an amplification of the effects of these chemicals. Blaszczynski, Winter, and McConaghy (1984) found that a group of pathological gamblers did not differ significantly from controls on baseline B-endorphin levels. However, by differentiating gamblers according to types of gambling, their research revealed that horse-racing gamblers had significantly lower levels of endorphins than poker-machine players. This suggests that the continuous activity inherent in playing poker machines may influence endorphin levels, as opposed to the sporadic gambling activity associated with horse-racing.

To date, the research appears to indicate that physiological factors play a role in the maintenance of pathological gambling. However, the exact nature of the role is still undetermined, and it is evident that considerably more research is required to isolate specific variables.

11

Psychological Features of Pathological Gamblers and Alcoholics

The two previous chapters describe the psychological and physical factors that sustain both alcoholism and pathological gambling. This chapter deals with the psychological characteristics of alcoholics and pathological gamblers.

Regardless of the type of addiction, most addicts manifest common personality attributes. In my book (1992), I describe personality characteristics that are common to most drug addicts, regardless of the specific drugs of preference, including alcohol. This chapter compares the psychological characteristics of alcoholics and pathological gamblers, noting substantial similarities, as well as a few differences. The characteristics described in this chapter apply to individuals who are still active in their drinking or gambling. When alcoholics and pathological gamblers arrest their harmful habits and begin recovery, these attributes of addiction gradually diminish, thus allowing for the emergence of normal functioning.

Need for Immediate Gratification

Both alcoholics and pathological gamblers are oriented toward having their needs satisfied immediately. Because drinking and gambling are both positively and negatively reinforcing, habitual drinkers and gamblers become dependent upon instant gratification, in concert with the immediate elimination of discomfort. Kissin (1977) believes that the reward of a sense of well-being and euphoria, or the relief of tension, are key components in the development of a powerful primary psychological addiction. This certainly applies to both alcoholics and pathological gamblers. When these individuals arrest their addictions, they must learn to accept delayed gratification. They must face and deal with reality, as unpleasant as it sometimes is, rather than habitually seeking instant escape.

The need for immediate gratification which is so characteristic of active alcoholism and pathological gambling, is remarkably similar to that of young children. Typically, most children have difficulty waiting for the proper time and place to have their needs satisfied. Consequently, an immature pattern of functioning, similar to that of children, is a natural outgrowth of alcoholism and pathological gambling.

Immaturity

Several features are characteristic of immature behavior. One is the need for immediate gratification, as described above. This need is problematic if it is powerful and if the individual acts without considering potential harmful consequences. Both alcoholics and pathological gamblers are plagued by a history of trouble secondary to their addictive habits. Both opt for immediate gratification without considering the results. Consequently, the behavior of alcoholics and pathological gamblers appears governed by impulsiveness. If these individuals were to seriously consider the harmful effects, they might choose not to drink or gamble. It is well established that pathological gamblers give the positive consequences of gambling priority over the harmful consequences (Ainslie 1984). With any addiction, the habit of opting for immediate relief, without regard for the harmful effects, is well entrenched.

Another feature of immaturity is low tolerance for stress. Alcoholics and pathological gamblers respond poorly to stress. By using alcohol consumption or gambling as a means of stress reduction, these individuals loose any effective coping skills, through lack of practice, that they may have had. Also as a function of their upbringing, many alcoholics and pathological gamblers have not learned effective coping skills in the first place (Kissin 1977; Custer and Milt 1985). Therefore, habitual drinking or gambling only functions to exacerbate the situation.

Case Examples

Joe began consuming alcohol in his early teens. By the time he was in his mid-twenties, Joe was showing signs of alcoholism including drinking considerably more than he should have, experiencing bouts of temporary amnesia when under the influence of alcohol, and drinking at inappropriate times and places. As a consequence, Joe has experienced difficulties with the law, has had broken relationships, and he has lost several jobs.

When Joe is employed, he frequently arrives late for work, and sometimes he even misses work, all because of his drinking. When challenged by an employer, Joe is known to overreact, and he has sometimes walked off the job. When Joe feels stressed at work, or if he does not get his way, he is irritable thus alienating himself from his co-workers. Joe acts similarly in relationships, alienating himself from a girlfriend on more than one occasion.

* * *

Martha is a heavy gambler. However, so far she has managed to keep her gambling and her gambling losses, a secret from others. This has not been an easy task, and it has resulted in a lot of lying, on Martha's part. Under continuous stress from trying to keep her gambling hidden and worried about her deteriorating financial situation, Martha is very temperamental. Day-to-day stressors that are relatively innocuous, usually cause Martha to overreact. Seeking immediate relief, Martha gambles even more.

On top of poor coping skills, alcoholics and pathological gamblers face above average stress, as a consequence of the problems caused by their drinking or gambling. Family, employment, financial, and legal difficulties add up to a lifestyle plagued by stress. This, in combination with poor coping skills, results in low tolerance for stress.

Defensiveness

Active alcoholics and pathological gamblers are committed to maintaining their respective addictions. When not drinking or gambling, they are often preoccupied with thoughts of doing so.

They cannot see living without their drinking or gambling. Consequently, when these individuals are challenged, they respond defensively. Rather than admitting that their drinking or gambling is a problem, they are evasive, argumentative, and make up excuses. When pushed, some promise that they'll cut back or quit, but these promises are usually short-lived. Alcoholics and pathological gamblers do everything that they can to hide their drinking or gambling and will deny that a problem exists. Excuse-making and rationalization are key elements of the defensive system of these individuals.

Abstinence forces these individuals to deal with lifestyles plagued by problems. This reality is very uncomfortable, causing the alcoholic or pathological gambler to resort to what he or she knows best. Alcoholics and pathological gamblers rely upon their respective habits as the only viable method of eliminating discomfort. Seeing no alternative, it is no wonder that they are compelled to defend against any challenge.

Case Example

Harvey is an accountant in private practice. He also drinks and gambles. During the early years of his alcohol consumption, Harvey's drinking was occasional and moderate and usually restricted to social situations. However, slowly and almost unnoticeably, Harvey's consumption of alcohol has increased to the point where he now drinks several times a week and usually to significant intoxication. Further, even though Harvey won't admit it, once he begins drinking he usually has trouble stopping.

About three years ago, Harvey began gambling. Now, Harvey is gambling several times a week, and his losses are considerably more than his winnings. It is not unusual for Harvey to drink and gamble at the same time. This, of course, adds recklessness to any gambling strategy that Harvey attempts to employ.

Due to his drinking and gambling habits, Harvey often arrives late for appointments with clients, and he even misses meetings. Because Harvey is frequently "hung over" from his drinking, and because he is distracted by financial worries due to ever-mounting gambling losses, Harvey is not as attentive as he should be to his clients. Consequently, Harvey's practice is in a slump. Also, all is not well in Harvey's marriage. Basically, Harvey's behavior toward his wife is a carbon-copy of that toward his clients.

On occasion, when Harvey's wife expresses her concerns regarding his drinking and gambling, Harvey responds angrily, giving his wife the message that, were she more understanding, he would not do what he does. Hearing this message repeatedly, Harvey's wife is beginning to believe that perhaps she does play a role in her husband's drinking and gambling. Feeling responsible for her husband's behavior, Harvey's wife acts in a very controlled manner towards him, hoping not to upset her husband.

Changes in Personality

As alcoholism and pathological gambling become progressively worse, afflicted individuals experience changes in personality. In the case of alcoholism, alcoholics usually feel regret for how they had behaved while under the influence, provided they are able to recall the events. In some cases, alcoholics experience bouts of temporary amnesia secondary to alcohol intoxication in which they have no subsequent recall of how they had behaved. Due to the lack of memory, alcoholics are often suspicious when confronted with their behavior, believing that their challengers are either exaggerating or lying. Eventually, suspiciousness becomes entrenched in an alcoholic's personality, and tends to wane only with permanent sobriety.

As a consequence of a dysfunctional lifestyle, alcoholics are plagued by anxiety, depression, and frequently insomnia. This discomfort precipitates further drinking, thus perpetuating the cycle. To avoid trouble, alcoholics attempt, albeit unsuccessfully, to control their alcohol consumption. This attempt at control usually generalizes, such that alcoholics blame and argue with others. To avoid provoking the alcoholic, people around the individual, especially family members, are swept up in trying to control their own behavior. This control cannot be sustained, and consequently the families of alcoholics are characterized by intermittent crises.

For the pathological gambler, personality changes are equally dysfunctional. Attempting to hide their gambling and the losses from gambling, pathological gamblers are increasingly irritable, critical, antagonistic, and impatient. However, the gambler is not always this way. In response to occasional wins, the gambler shows bouts of pleasantness. However, these nice periods do not last long. In response to inevitable losses, the individual manifests renewed irritability and hostility. This flip-flop in behavior is very confusing for family members. As the gambling progresses, bouts of depression and anxiety are increasingly frequent. Like the alcoholic, the pathological gambler assigns blame to others, most specifically members of his or her family.

Mood Swings

It is common for alcoholics and pathological gamblers to have mood swings. Alcoholics frequently experience anger, guilt, and depression in response to drinking-related problems. More drinking may temporarily lift an individual's mood or, alternatively, it may release hostility and aggression. Therefore, on one day an alcoholic may be remorseful and repentant, and on the next day blaming and angry. Similarly, a pathological gambler may be jubilant in response to a big win, and the next day angry and remorseful in response to a loss. Because alcoholics and pathological gamblers are defensive and suspicious, they frequently overreact to seemingly trivial events. This paints an overall picture of unpredictability in mood.

Given that alcoholism and pathological gambling cause so many problems, it is difficult to comprehend why alcoholics and pathological gamblers are so persistent in maintaining their dysfunctional lifestyles. The answer lies in two processes that work in tandem. First, in the vast majority of cases, alcoholics do not consume alcohol with the express intent of creating problems. Nor do pathological gamblers gamble with the express intent of losing money. Both engage in their respective habits for immediate pleasure and relief, and in the case of gambling, to win money. Unfortunately, harmful consequences follow, which in turn activates the second process. Because alcoholics and pathological gamblers are so dependent upon immediate gratification, they are in a mental state that psychologically isolates their drinking or gambling from the subsequent problems. This mental state is called denial.

Denial

Denial is a way of thinking that prevents an individual from recognizing thoughts, emotions, and events that create excessive anxiety. Denial occurs automatically and usually at a level below awareness. In other words, an individual in denial is not aware that he or she is denying. Denial may be beneficial, in that it blocks the mind from recognizing certain thoughts, memories, or feelings, which if conscious, could create overwhelming anxiety. For example, some individuals who have been sexually abused have no recall of the events. Denial keeps the memories out of consciousness, usually until the individual is emotionally stable enough to deal with them. In other cases, denial is overbearing, thus preventing the individual from recognizing what is required to resolve a problem. In many cases, denial prevents the person from recognizing that a problem exists. With alcoholism and pathological gambling, this is typically the case.

Alcoholics in a state of denial are convinced that they can control their alcohol consumption and therefore, drink safely. This manner of thinking prevents the alcoholic from recognizing the connection between drinking and subsequent problems. In denial, the alcoholic believes that the problems have causes other than drinking. Because alcoholics are so committed to drinking, thoughts of quitting create anxiety. Consequently, denial protects them from the anxiety associated with thoughts of abstinence. Denial fools people into believing that they do not need to stop drinking.

Case Example

Daniel made an appointment to see a psychologist, because Daniel was worried about his wife's threats to separate from him. Daniel claimed that his wife is concerned about how much alcohol he consumes. However, Daniel made it clear to the doctor that he did not have a problem with alcohol. Daniel explained that he couldn't possibility be an alcoholic, because he doesn't drink every day, he's been consistently employed, he's never had any trouble with the law, and he's always taken care of his family.

When Daniel was asked why his wife believes that he has a problem with alcohol, Daniel explained that his wife grew up in an alcoholic family. Both of his wife's parents had consumed alcohol heavily. However, Daniel went on to explain that his in-laws are now sober, and, according to him, they are seeing "an alcoholic behind every tree." He claims that his in-laws are influencing his wife, such that she now believes that he is an alcoholic.

When asked to describe his marriage, Daniel talked about how in the early days, his marriage had been good. He and his wife shared feelings with one another, they often went out together, they had a good sexual relationship, and so on. Daniel then went on to describe how his marriage had slowly deteriorated. He talked about how his wife no longer shares her feelings with him, refuses to go out with him, and doesn't want to be sexually involved with him. By the time Daniel was finished talking, there were tears in his eyes. Daniel obviously loves his wife, and he blames her parents for his marriage problems.

After hearing about Daniel's marriage, the psychologist asked Daniel about his alcohol consumption.

Daniel's drinking history revealed that, when he first began drinking, he would go with a few of his friends to a bar after work, on Friday evenings. Daniel would have a few drinks, and then come home and spend the rest of the evening with his wife. On the weekends, Daniel and his wife would attend social events, and Daniel would have a few drinks. In other words, in the early days of his marriage, Daniel's alcohol consumption was occasional and light.

However, Daniel quickly discovered that a few drinks would quickly eliminate any tension that had built up over the week, and, in social situations, Daniel relied upon alcohol to help him socialize more easily. Over the years, to achieve these effects, Daniel consumed increasingly greater amounts of alcohol, mainly on weekends. He rarely drank during the week.

Currently, Daniel still goes to the bar after work, on Friday evenings, with his friends. However, the situation is now different. Even though Daniel intends to have just a few drinks, he drinks considerably more than a few, and he often comes home quite intoxicated, thus not following through with any plans that he may have made with his wife. Further, when under the influence of alcohol, Daniel is belligerent toward his wife. On several occasions, while under the influence of alcohol, Daniel has embarrassed his wife in social situations. Also, whenever he comes home and is drunk, Daniel wants to have sex with his wife, and he becomes angry when she does not respond.

When the psychologist later met with Daniel and his wife, it was readily apparent that whenever Daniel's wife expresses her concerns about Daniel's drinking, he blames her and accuses her of exaggerating and of making up stories. Because Daniel sometimes experiences bouts of alcohol-induced temporary amnesia, he does not recall some of his behavior toward his wife, and accuses her of lying.

Daniel is in a state of denial. He genuinely believes that he does not have a problem with alcohol, and that his wife does not understand him. Reality contradicts him.

The process is the same for pathological gamblers. Despite excessive losses and the poor odds of getting ahead, these individuals convince themselves that they are only one chance away from a big win. For this type of gambler, reality is fraught with anxiety. Reality would force the gambler to deal with his or her losses. To avoid the overwhelming anxiety associated with reality, the gambler clings to a protective state of denial.

Case Example

Susan is a 55-year-old widow who lives alone, supported by her deceased husband's pension. Susan's husband died eight years ago from cancer. Susan has three children, all living away from home, and she has many friends. Since her husband's death, Susan has taken to gambling, mainly at a local casino. At first, Susan restricted her gambling losses to a certain amount, leaving the casino when she had reached her limit. If she had a significant win, Susan would stop gambling on that particular day. However, during the last several years, Susan has found herself gambling more frequently, for larger stakes, and for longer periods of time. As a matter of fact, on quite a few occasions, Susan found herself gambling and losing track of time. As a consequence, by the time she realizes how much she has gambled, Susan's losses are significant. The result is that Susan has run into debt, borrowing money from a variety of sources, including her daughters.

With mounting gambling losses, unable to pay down her debts, and running short of money for basics, Susan was caught forging checks against her children's bank accounts. Despite her troubles, Susan continues to gamble. When Susan's lawyer referred her to a psychologist for an assessment for court, and when the psychologist had asked Susan if she believed that she had a problem with gambling, Susan recognized that gambling was a problem, but her solution is to continue gambling, on the assumption that a big win, which would solve her financial problems, was imminent.

Susan is in denial. Even though she recognizes that gambling has resulted in problems for her, she is convinced that continued gambling is her salvation. Despite the odds against coming out ahead, and despite her history of losses, Susan persists in gambling.

Occasionally, problems become so overwhelming that denial suddenly breaks down, leaving the alcoholic or the pathological gambler fully exposed and vulnerable. When this happens, the individual is in crisis, is overpowered by emotion, and sometimes becomes suicidal. Typically, it is at this time that many people approach treatment. Others seek refuge by gambling or drinking more heavily than ever, and some attempt suicide.

Denial is a basic psychological process manifested by characteristic thinking. Walters (1994) refers to types of thinking that reflect denial. Although Walters refers specifically to pathological gambling when describing these ways of thinking, the thinking also applies to alcoholism.

The first way of thinking described by Walters is called *mollification*. Pathological gamblers who think in this manner tend to minimize the significance of gambling in their lifestyles. They rationalize that gambling is socially condoned, popular, and a few problems here and there are of no significance. Any type of excuse that people use to explain away the harmful consequences of their gambling is mollification. Walters gives the example of bingo players explaining their losses as not being harmful, because the money goes to charity. Blaming gambling on stress, or blaming another person for one's gambling are other examples. Alcoholics also engage in mollification by finding reasons to condone their drinking, making up excuses for why they drink, and so on.

Entitlement is another way of thinking that reflects denial, and which as described by Walters, leads pathological gamblers to believe that they are entitled to gamble because they are different. According to Walters, these individuals give themselves permission to gamble, because they believe that they deserve special consideration. This type of thinking is also common among alcoholics. Alcoholics will often consume alcohol under the impression that they do not deserve to feel anxiety, depression, or any other uncomfortable emotion.

A natural outgrowth of entitlement thinking is the persistence of pathological gamblers and alcoholics in negotiating with reality. They make abstinence contingent upon the absence of stress. When stress inevitably occurs, alcoholics and pathological gamblers rebel by engaging in their addictive habits.

The third way of thinking described by Walters is *sentimentality* and is common for both pathological gamblers and alcoholics. For example, a pathological gambler buys loved ones something expensive with his or her winnings to compensate them for the problems associated with gambling. Alcoholics also attempt to compensate with a repentant attitude, gifts, and so on.

Walters refers to *superoptimism,* the fourth way of thinking, as a false belief that one can continually postpone problems. According to Walters, this type of thinking is the basis of the *chasing* behavior of the pathological gambler in which the individual attempts to make up for losses with further gambling, under the assumption that the next chance will result in a big win. Alcoholics also engage in superoptimism. Despite a history of drinking-related problems, they still harbor the belief that, "this time it will be different."

Hypercompetitiveness, the fifth way, a particular type of thinking described by Walters, is more characteristic of pathological gamblers than of alcoholics. This thinking reflects an extreme competitiveness on behalf of the gambler to beat the odds. This obsessiveness to beat the odds and the excitement associated with occasionally beating the odds is so powerful that it takes precedent over family, friends, and financial security. According to Walters, the excitement of beating the odds rivals the euphoria associated with drug use.

In my book (1995), I describe a way of thinking that like those described by Walters, also reflects denial. I refer to this thinking as *euphoric recall,* which occurs when alcoholics and pathological gamblers selectively recall the good times associated with drinking or gambling and effectively ignore the bad times. They use euphoric recall to persuade themselves that good days are ahead, and that they are able to drink or gamble safely.

The more involved an individual is with gambling, the more likely the person is to believe that his or her particular gambling behavior will affect the outcome (Griffiths 1993). This type of thinking is defined as the *illusion of control* (Langer 1975). Illusions of control occur with both pathological gamblers and alcoholics. Research indicates that alcoholics believe that they can control their drinking, and they have more positive expectations of what drinking will do for them, than light drinkers (Christiansen and Brown 1985). Similar evidence indicates that pathological gamblers have unrealistic positive expectations regarding the outcome of their gambling. Pathological gamblers also tend to overrate their skill in gambling, as well as the positive effects of gambling (Griffiths 1990).

It is evident that all of these unhealthy reasoning patterns allow people to fool themselves into believing that they do not have a problem with either alcohol consumption or gambling. Denial, in all of its various manifestations, allows individuals to isolate their drinking or gambling from the problems that these activities cause.

12
Progression of Pathological Gambling and Alcoholism

Pathological gambling and alcoholism are not static conditions. Unless afflicted individuals arrest their disorders, they will become progressively worse. If alcoholism, in particular, is not checked, it may result in premature death. One of the most common causes of premature death among alcoholics is suicide. Studies indicate that the risk of suicide among alcoholics is thirty times greater than the general population (National Institute on Alcohol Abuse and Alcoholism 1982). Another common cause of premature death among alcoholics, arises from the physical problems associated with heavy drinking. Other causes of death include accidents and in some cases, violence. Pathological gamblers are also at risk. Evidence indicates that 20 percent of pathological gamblers make at least one attempt at suicide (Rosenthal 1992).

People do not begin gambling or drinking with the intent of developing a dependence. Most individuals who consume alcohol and/or gamble, manage to restrict these activities to appropriate occasions and places. For reasons that are not fully understood, some develop into pathological gamblers, and others into alcoholics. Some who like both gambling and drinking, develop problems with both.

This chapter deals with the stages of progression of pathological gambling and of alcoholism. Although the rate of progressive deterioration for either disorder varies from person to person, and although not everyone experiences the same difficulties, there are common characteristics.

Progression of Pathological Gambling

Rosenthal (1992) describes four stages of progression. Although pathological gamblers and social gamblers may start out the same, the subsequent gambling pattern of the latter is relatively static, whereas the pattern of the former is progressive.

Stage One — The Winning Stage

During this stage of gambling, people gamble because they enjoy the activity. Because it occurs early in a gambler's betting career, losses are not considered a problem. For people who are predisposed to developing gambling problems, a few significant wins here and there function to establish gambling as an important pastime. While social gamblers enjoy winning, wins do not have the same significance, in terms of elevating the importance of gambling. Even though losses may be greater than wins, during this stage, predisposed individuals are psychologically oriented toward wins, and they trivialize losses. While most predisposed men at this stage gamble for the excitement and the challenge and because winning builds their self-esteem (Rosenthal 1992), the evidence suggests that the majority of women who develop into pathological gamblers begin gambling as a means of escape (Lesieur and Blume 1991).

The type of gambling engaged in by women at this stage, differs from men. Most women enjoy card games, bingo, slot machines, and lotteries, while the majority of men enjoy horse racing, sports betting, and games involving dice (Lesieur and Blume 1991). Women prefer to gamble at games with a high probability of at least some monetary return, whereas men prefer games with a high return, even if the probability of winning is low (Bruce and Johnson 1994). While most men who become pathological gamblers begin their gambling careers early in life, usually as adolescents, the majority of women begin gambling after they have become adults, often in response to depression (Rosenthal 1992). Regardless of their reasons for gambling, sooner or later the losses from gambling prevail, and people find themselves in the second stage.

Stage Two — The Losing Stage

It is during this stage that losses become significant. Losing can no longer be trivialized, because losses are such that they result in significant discomfort. This leads to the chasing behavior (Rosenthal 1992). Gamblers become obsessed with returning to gambling, to win back their losses. In a panic, the gambler abandons previous strategies for gambling. At this stage, the individual experiences a sense of urgency, and bets are placed more frequently. In response to accumulating losses, the gambler lies and makes up excuses for money that has "disappeared."

During this stage, men converge with women by gambling for escape. The Pathological Gambling Cycle is now entrenched. Individuals gamble to relieve themselves of unpleasant feelings. However, more losses occur, and the losses are followed by more unpleasant feelings. Occasional wins function to provide the gambler with a sense of false hope that a solution is imminent. According to Lesieur and Blume (1991, p.186), "Those who are escaping from some problem comment on gambling as an *anesthetic* which *hypnotizes.*" While gambling, the individual is in a mental state which Jacobs (1988) refers to as *dissociative.*

Eventually, time spent gambling, the mood swings, and the financial losses take their toll, causing problems in the family and on the job. Wexler (1981) and Custer and Milt (1985) found that spouses of pathological gamblers at first deny that a problem exists. The same frequently happens with employers and business partners. When gambling problems are eventually exposed, the gambler is usually provided financial assistance by family and friends. This "bail-out" (Rosenthal 1992) often functions to give the gambler renewed confidence in his or her abilities to overcome the "odds." Despite the gamblers promises to quit, the confidence produced by the bail-out often propels the individual into further gambling. Eventually the problems become so significant, that pathological gamblers lose their families and jobs.

Stage Three — The Desperation Stage

This stage of progression is characterized by the gambler engaging in activities which would not have been considered previously. For example, to acquire money with which to gamble, many individuals resort to criminal activity, such as writing bad checks, forgery, and embezzlement. Rather than recognizing this behavior for what it is, the gambler will rationalize the activity as a loan and fully intend to make restitution — with a big win. However, further gambling losses usually make restitution impossible. The stress associated with criminal activity, along with the fear of being caught, results in feelings of irritability, suspiciousness, and anger.

Stage Four — The Hopelessness Stage

In this stage, the pathological gambler stops caring. The person gambles to detach from reality. The individual gambles for hours or sometimes days at a time. By now, everyone is aware that a significant problem exists, and sometimes intervention by family or employers propel the gambler into treatment. In other cases, the person seeks treatment voluntarily. Still, suicide attempts are common (Rosenthal 1992).

Case Example

Tim first began gambling as a teen-ager. At the beginning, Tim's gambling was restricted to the occasional card game and sometimes to betting on sporting events. However, because he liked the activity, Tim was soon gambling more frequently. Because he worked at a part-time job on weekends, while attending high school, Tim had sufficient amounts of money with which to gamble. A few significant wins here and there established gambling as an important pastime for Tim. Before he knew it, Tim was gambling regularly.

Tim enjoyed gambling for two reasons. First, he found the activity exciting, and second, Tim liked to gamble because his friends did. However, there was a difference between Tim and his friends. While most of Tim's friends gambled occasionally, Tim was a regular gambler, gambling at least once or twice a week.

Tim graduated from high school, and he attended university. Tim's goal was to become an architect. At university, one of Tim's main social activities was gambling. Besides gambling at card games and sporting events, Tim enjoyed going to casinos. While attending university, Tim met and dated his wife-to-be. By the time Tim graduated from architecture, he was married.

Soon after graduation, Tim accepted a position with a local architecture firm. Because Tim and his wife were both employed, they had considerable disposable income.

During the early days of Tim's marriage, life was good. Tim enjoyed his job, he and his wife were compatible, and he was earning a substantial income. Before he knew it, Tim found himself gambling more frequently and for longer periods. To achieve a desired level of excitement, Tim also began increasing the size of his bets.

Over the next several years, Tim gambled more frequently and heavily. As a consequence, gambling losses were becoming significant. Much of Tim's disposable income was directed toward gambling and paying down his losses. Gambling was no longer as enjoyable as it had been. Following his losses, which were becoming more frequent, Tim had strong urges to return to the casinos to make up for the losses.

As Tim's gambling losses mounted, and because Tim was spending much of his free time gambling, Tim's wife began to express concern. Arguments occurred, and Tim made major efforts to hide both his gambling and his losses from his wife. This included lying to his wife about where he spent much of his time and making up excuses about why he was always short of money. However, Tim was not successful in keeping his gambling a secret , and arguments between him and his wife escalated.

On a few occasions, Tim had big wins. This prompted Tim to buy his wife some expensive gifts, which temporarily appeased her. However, continuing losses contributed toward more marital strife. Going further into debt, Tim took a second mortgage out on his house, and he pawned some of his wife's expensive jewelry. When Tim's wife found out about this, she separated from him. Tim was devastated by the separation, and he solemnly promised his wife that he would quit gambling. This prompted his wife to move back home.

Tim maintained his promise of abstinence for a few months. However, during this period, Tim was irritable, feeling as if something was missing from his life. In response, Tim decided to gamble, but to restrict his gambling to once per week. However, within a few weeks, Tim was gambling more heavily than prior to the marriage separation. Tim was so controlled by gambling that he missed work, was constantly preoccupied with his deteriorating financial situation, irritable toward coworkers when he did attend, and Tim's job performance deteriorated.

Tim lost his marriage about the same time that he lost his home. Depressed and feeling hopeless and very alone, Tim threw himself into gambling. By now, he didn't care whether he won or lost. All that Tim knew was that as long as he was gambling, he did not think about his problems. Missing work and performing poorly when he was there, Tim's job was soon added to his other losses.

Progressive Deterioration for Alcoholism

In my book (1989), I describe the three stages of alcoholism as the early, middle, and late stages. Like pathological gambling, it usually takes a number of years before family members and others, recognize that a person has a problem with drinking. Even then, it usually takes a few more years before anything significant is done about it. Consequently, most alcoholics have progressed through at least two stages before they do something about their drinking. Some never quit until they die prematurely. This chapter describes the common characteristics of the progressive deterioration of alcoholism.

The Early Stage

In this stage, alcoholism is not easily recognized. There are, however, several indicators that suggest that a problem exists. Early-stage alcoholics show evidence of becoming increasingly preoccupied with drinking. They prefer to attend events where alcohol is present. If alcohol isn't present, alcoholics frequently fortify themselves by drinking before the event. The person also shows increased tolerance where more alcohol is now required to produce an effect. The individual's alcohol consumption is now marked by a loss of control, and the person does not seem to know when to stop drinking. However, the situation is not one of not knowing when to stop, but rather one of being unable to stop. Consequently, a drinking pattern of continuous daily consumption or alternatively, binge drinking, evolves. Temporary amnesic episodes or blackouts sometimes occur (although not all alcoholics experience blackouts). A blackout occurs when an alcoholic is consuming alcohol, and has no recall of what transpires.

From an emotional perspective, the early-stage alcoholic is defensive about drinking, especially when challenged. The person becomes secretive, denies consuming alcohol, and makes up excuses. Further, alcoholics often blame others for their drinking. Drinking-related employment problems, arguments with family or friends, fights, legal charges, and so on, occur. Occasionally, family, friends, or coworkers shield the alcoholic from the consequences of his or her drinking. This is referred to as enabling and strengthens the alcoholic's denial.

In response to drinking-related problems, alcoholics promise to moderate or quit drinking. When these promises break down, as they usually do, alcoholics find themselves drinking more than ever. This brings the alcoholic to the middle-stage of alcoholism.

Middle Stage

It is during this stage that withdrawal or detoxification symptoms become evident. Alcoholics find themselves drinking to prevent the distress of alcohol withdrawal. To avoid the agony of withdrawal, many alcoholics maintain a pattern of continuous daily drinking, which often includes morning drinking. For others who binge, their benders are now frequent and longer. Drinking episodes may vary from days to several weeks. Typically, blackouts are more frequent and last longer. In some cases, blackouts may persist for several days. The alcoholic is now firmly entrenched in the Alcoholism Drinking Cycle. The individual drinks to avoid the stress of withdrawal and to forget the problems caused by drinking.

Due to mounting problems, thoughts of suicide and perhaps attempts, are more frequent. For some individuals, alcohol-related physical problems, including severe withdrawal, result in hospitalizations. Others are hospitalized for alcohol-precipitated psychiatric problems. During this stage, many alcoholics lose or quit their jobs, marriages fall apart, and financial and legal difficulties occur. Having lost control over how much alcohol they consume, individuals in this stage also lose control over when and where they drink. Those who do not quit drinking become progressively worse.

Late Stage

Physical symptoms are increasingly evident during this stage. For some, withdrawal reactions are now so severe that hallucinations and convulsive seizures occur. Chronic drinking also results in diseases of the liver and other organs. Some alcoholics show indications of brain damage caused by heavy drinking. Accidents result in bruises, cuts, bone fractures, and sometimes death. Because alcohol is an analgesic, alcoholics often do not feel pain. Consequently, many are unaware of how sick they really are. Among those who are aware of the severity of their problems, many give up caring for themselves. Premature death is common.

Case Example

Larry began drinking when he was sixteen years old. He enjoyed the feeling associated with alcohol consumption. Drinking on weekends became a regular part of Larry's life, and he was frequently intoxicated. During

Larry's senior year in high school, he was having blackouts when he drank. However, he considered them a joke and so did his friends.

After graduating from high school, Larry attended college and then Law School. While at college, Larry met and dated his wife-to-be. During his college and Law School years, Larry restricted his drinking to weekend evenings. However, on these occasions, Larry always became very intoxicated. While many of Larry's classmates also got drunk, there were differences between Larry's alcohol consumption and that of the others. While each of Larry's friends occasionally became drunk, Larry was the one who was regularly intoxicated. He was also the one who could not recall what had happened when he was drinking and the one who always needed help getting home. During his college years, Larry also discovered that he had to consume increasingly greater amounts of alcohol in order to become intoxicated. Consequently, Larry developed a reputation for being able to hold his liquor.

Despite his heavy alcohol consumption during weekends, Larry graduated from college, and then law school. Upon graduating from law school and passing his bar exams, Larry was offered a junior position at a law firm. Shortly after, Larry was married.

Larry soon realized that drinking was a way of life for his colleagues. There were many social functions to attend and clients to wine and dine. However, Larry's style of drinking was different from that of the other lawyers. His lifestyle included consuming cocktails at lunch and having a few drinks at home, after work. Before retiring to bed, Larry would have a few more drinks. On weekends, Larry drank considerably more alcohol, and his bouts of temporary amnesia were more frequent and more extensive. However, Larry was now used to having blackouts, and he considered them a normal part of drinking.

By the time Larry was forty, he was offered a partnership in the law firm. He had three children and lived in a large home in a nice residential area. Larry was successful at his work, and he believed he was on his way to the top.

About this time, Larry's wife became concerned about her husband's drinking. She noticed that his alcohol consumption had increased significantly. He became rude and belligerent when under the influence, and he frequently had no recall of how he had behaved. Further, Larry was becoming increasingly preoccupied with drinking and showed less interest in his wife and children. In response to his wife's concern regarding his drinking, Larry was angry, accusing her of exaggeration and of making up stories. Regardless, Larry promised his wife that he would moderate his alcohol consumption.

Larry's attempt at moderation lasted only for a few weeks. It ended one day when Larry stopped at a bar, on the way home from work. Even though he intended to have only a couple of drinks, Larry had considerably more, and he arrived home late that evening, very much under the influence of alcohol. As a consequence, Larry's wife took the children and moved in with her parents.

Over the next several months, Larry's alcohol consumption was heavy and daily. As a consequence, his performance at work deteriorated significantly. He also took extended lunch breaks, returning to work in mid-afternoons with the noticeable odor of alcohol on his breath. In response, Larry's partners found themselves covering for him. After awhile, they decided to confront Larry about his drinking, and he promised to stop.

Larry honored his promise for about six months. During this time, Larry and his wife reconciled, and his performance at work improved significantly. However, Larry missed drinking. In response, he decided that he would resume his alcohol consumption, but that he would maintain control. Within a month of this experiment, Larry went on an alcohol bender, which resulted in him disappearing for several days. In response, Larry's partners bought him out, and his wife filed for divorce.

Unemployed and alone, Larry moved into an apartment and proceeded to live off of the savings from the buy-out. It only took Larry two years to drink away his savings. During this time, he moved into progressively cheaper living quarters and, eventually, Larry ended up living in a rooming house. On one occasion, Larry was in a detoxification unit. On two occasions Larry got into bar fights, and he was beaten up.

Because Larry doesn't eat well, wash, or shave very often, he looks sickly, unkempt, and older than his age. Larry is continuously intoxicated, and at night he falls into fitful sleeps. Sometimes, prior to falling asleep, Larry hears the voices of his children admonishing him. Thoughts of suicide are occurring more frequently.

13

Social Signs of Alcoholism and Pathological Gambling

Both alcoholism and pathological gambling are progressive disorders. If left unchecked, both can result in a vast array of difficulties, many of which are evident at a social level.

Alcohol consumption and gambling are popular in western society. Some cultures within the North American society even condone heavy drinking and gambling. Consequently, the signs of alcoholism and pathological gambling are often considered inconsequential in groups where heavy gambling and drinking are the norm. If the majority of individuals in a particular culture either drink or gamble in a harmful manner, this behavior may be considered typical, and therefore not generate much concern. This does not imply that alcoholism and pathological gambling do not exist in these groups, but rather that the social signs of either disorder are not easily distinguishable from what is usual. This chapter focuses on the social indicators of alcoholism and pathological gambling.

Family Problems

For years, alcoholism has been recognized as a major disrupter of family harmony. The *Fifth Special Report to the U.S. Congress on Alcohol and Health* (1983) states that the rate of marital separation and divorce for alcoholics, is seven times greater than that of the general population. The Report also states that 40 percent of family court problems involve alcoholism.

The harmful impact of pathological gambling upon the family closely parallels that of alcoholism. For instance, Ciarrocchi and Hohmann (1989) found that both alcoholics and pathological gamblers show high levels of dissatisfaction with their family environments. Pathological gambling is known to create severe marital problems (Lesieur 1984; Lorenz and Yaffe 1986). The families of pathological gamblers are typically in distress caused by anger, physical violence, harassment by bill collectors, and by suicide threats and attempts on behalf of the gambler (Lorenz 1981; Lorenz and Shuttlesworth 1983).

Because alcoholism and pathological gambling have such a harmful impact upon the family, the next chapter deals exclusively with this topic.

Employment Problems

Poor work productivity is closely associated with alcoholism and pathological gambling. Both alcoholics and pathological gamblers experience employment difficulties due to absenteeism, coming to work late, distraction by worries, extended lunches, and irritability and moodiness. Additionally, drinking on the job is closely related to accidents at work. Research indicates that fatal accidents are more likely to happen to people who drink while at work, as opposed to those who do not (*Fifth Special Report to the U.S. Congress on Alcohol and Health* 1983). Shain (1982) found that alcoholics are two to three times more likely to experience work-related accidents than nonalcoholics. These results are not unexpected, given the relationship between alcohol consumption, impaired judgment, and loss of control over motor coordination.

Other Accidents

Besides accidents at work, alcoholics are more likely to be involved in traffic accidents, than are nondrinkers or light drinkers (Fell 1982). Despite widespread education about the potentially harmful consequences of drinking and driving, many individuals still persist in driving while under the influence of alcohol. Most people believe that they are impaired only if they are drunk. They are not aware that even relatively small amounts of alcohol impairs both judgment and coordination. In the case of many alcoholics, high tolerance allows them to consume considerable amounts of alcohol and not feel drunk. This provides them with the illusion that they are not impaired, when the opposite is true.

Besides traffic and work accidents, alcoholism is highly correlated with home and recreational accidents. Studies indicate that alcoholics are at greater risk of dying from falls, than are nonalcoholics (Brenner 1967; Schmidt and de Lint 1972). Schmidt and de Lint also found that alcoholics are more likely to die in fires. Alcoholics are at high risk for accidents, because heavy alcohol consumption impairs both physical coordination and judgment. Pathological gamblers are less likely to experience accidents because they do not suffer from impaired physical coordination.

Crime

Although many alcoholics do not engage in criminal activity, and although not all criminals are alcoholic, there is a significant relationship between alcoholism and crime (*Fifth Special Report to the U.S. Congress on Alcohol and Health* 1983), including murder, rape, and family violence. Heavy drinking results in a loss of emotional inhibition. When combined with impaired judgment, the loss of inhibition may result in criminal behavior. Pathological gambling also is associated with criminal behavior. Livingston (1974) found that pathological gambling may result in employee theft, forgery (mainly checks), embezzlement, and the selling of stolen material. Lesieur (1984) also found that a significant number of pathological gamblers are involved in fraud, tax evasion, prostitution, and pimping. As compared to alcoholics who tend to commit crimes against people, pathological gamblers usually commit crimes against property (Brown 1987).

14
Effects On the Family

Both alcoholism and pathological gambling have a negative influence upon the family, evidenced by a frequency of marriage breakdown that is higher than in the general population. This chapter deals with family processes, and the various harmful ways that these two disorders impact upon them.

Communication

Communication may be divided into two components: clarity and directness. Effective communication is usually clear and direct. Clear communication is characterized by messages that are unambiguous, and understandable. For example, "You wouldn't want to go out with me, would you?" is considerably less clear than, "Would you like to go out with me?"

Families of alcoholics and pathological gamblers are typically characterized by high levels of stress, and family members are usually defensive and unhappy. Because family members are often concerned about the alcoholic's or gambler's reactions, including drinking and/or gambling, they usually relate in an unclear manner, under the assumption that arguments may be avoided through ambiguity. For example, the husband of a pathological gambler wishes to speak with his wife about getting the family finances under control. Because he is unsure of how she will react, and because he does not want is wife to gamble, he hints around the topic, afraid to clearly express himself. His wife senses his insecurity, is resentful, and goes gambling. Although unclear communication appears to have an apparent protective value, it really contributes toward increasing stress levels in the family.

Besides relating in an unclear manner, members of an alcoholic's or a pathological gambler's family often relate indirectly with one another. Indirect communication occurs when one family member, afraid to speak with another, relays a message through a third member. Often the third member is a child. In the previous example, the husband, fearful of his wife's reaction, may relay a message to her through one of their children. This creates two problems. First, messages relayed *via* an intermediary usually become distorted, and second, children are often not mature enough to deal with the stress of relaying emotionally-laden messages. For example, the wife of an alcoholic is afraid to tell her husband that she does not wish to attend a social event with him, because in the past he has always become intoxicated, and he has frequently embarrassed her. Concerned about her husband's reaction if she was to tell him the truth, the wife asks her young son to tell his father that she cannot go out, because she has a headache. Her husband, sensing his wife's rejection, is angry and storms out of the house. Several hours later, he comes home very drunk. The boy blames himself both for his father's anger and for his father getting drunk.

Ineffective ways of relating with one another not only prevent families from solving problems, but they also add problems by contributing to stress levels in the family. However, family members feel stuck, because they are fearful of the consequences of relating directly and clearly.

Family Coalitions

A coalition is a group of people who identify with one another because they share a common identity. All families have coalitions. In healthy families, coalitions consist of parental groupings, and groupings of children. Even in healthy single-parent families, the children still form a coalition because of a common identity. The implicit function of the parental coalition is to conceive, protect, rear, and socialize the children.

Typically, the families of alcoholics and pathological gamblers are characterized by unhealthy coalitions. If the alcoholic or pathological gambler is a parent, the drinking or gambling weakens the parental coalition, and sometimes the coalition breaks down entirely. If both parents drink or gamble heavily, the situation is exaggerated. Due to their drinking or gambling, individuals become isolated from their families, even if they still reside in the same dwelling. Heavy drinking and/or gambling interferes with the person's involvement with members of his or her family, family members do not share their feelings with the alcoholic or gambler, and the drinker or gambler is often excluded from problem-solving discussions. If the drinker or gambler is a child (teen-ager), that individual is often isolated from both parents and siblings.

In situations where the parental coalition is weakened due to heavy drinking or gambling, the non-drinking or non-gambling spouse often over identifies with his or her children, and an unhealthy coalition develops. The drinking or gambling parent is underinvolved with the children, and the other parent is overinvolved. Often, the result is emotional and social isolation for the drinker or gambler, and the other spouse is overrelating with the children, in a manner which satisfies the needs of the spouse more than that of the children. This places unrealistic emotional demands upon the children. For example, in response to her heavy alcohol consumption, a man leaves his wife, and he relies almost exclusively upon his children to meet his loneliness. This places unfair demands upon his children, causing them to feel guilty about leaving their father alone, in order to spend time with their friends.

Roles Within a Family

Every family member, regardless of age, has implicit roles. The various roles of individual family members typically change in response to maturation. For example, the role of a baby is to be cared for. As the baby grows into a young child, his or her roles change. In healthy families, role change often occurs as result of discussion, and sometimes individual initiative. For example, a parent may decide that a child is now old enough to engage in various family chores, and a discussion subsequently occurs to initiate the process. Sometimes family members decide on their own to adopt new roles, or to assume roles that they previously did not fill. In order for a change in roles to be effective, members must feel comfortable relating with one another.

Because the families of alcoholics and pathological gamblers are characterized by ineffective communication and unhealthy coalitions, many roles are vaguely defined, and otherwise go unfilled. Also, family members are often unsure of which roles to fill. Because the drinker or gambler often relinquishes many of his or her roles, other family members are forced to fill the vacuum. A classic example is older children being forced to care for younger siblings, because a parent(s) is out drinking or gambling.

Enabling

Even though the members of families of alcoholics and pathological gamblers are unhappy, without knowing it, they sometimes unintentionally reinforce the drinking or gambling behavior of their alcoholic or pathological gambler. This is referred to as enabling, and it occurs when people drink or gamble with impunity, because others (usually family members, and sometimes coworkers or employers) protect these individuals from the harmful consequences of their drinking or gambling. For example, due to heavy gambling losses, an individual is faced with impending bankruptcy. His father, feeling sorry for him, offers to pay the gambler's debts. Or, an alcoholic who had been drinking heavily the previous evening, does not show up for work the next morning. Because a husband cares about his wife and doesn't want her to lose her job, he phones his wife's employer and explains that his wife is ill with the flu. In both cases, despite honorable intentions from others, the pathological gambler and the alcoholic are shielded from the harmful consequences of their behaviors.

Enabling occurs for a variety of reasons. In some cases, people cannot accept that a member of their family is an alcoholic or a pathological gambler. This may be due to embarrassment, guilt, or a variety of other reasons. Regardless, refusal to admit that a problem exists only strengthens the denial of the afflicted individual. Some family members even join in the drinking or gambling, believing that if they cannot beat them, they might as well join them. In other cases, family members blame themselves for an individual's drinking or gambling. They accept the accusations that it is their fault that the alcoholic drinks or that the gambler gambles. Alcoholics and pathological gamblers characteristically blame others for their problems, and when family members accept this blame, they relieve the alcoholic or the gambler of responsibility. Some family members try to keep the peace at any cost. Others protect their alcoholic or pathological gambler, because not doing so results in distress for the family. With reference to the above examples, if the father were to allow his son to declare bankruptcy, the father would feel bad. In the second case, the husband would experience financial hardship and guilt, if his wife were to lose her job.

Regardless of the reasons for enabling, it strengthens drinking or gambling behavior by absolving the individual of responsibility for the consequences of his or her drinking or gambling.

15
Recovery: Why Do People Stop Drinking or Gambling?

Pathological gambling and alcoholism result in distress for afflicted individuals, as well as for those around them. In the early stage of these disorders, people drink or gamble, because they like the effects, and they disregard the harmful consequences. Even as problems mount, pathological gamblers and alcoholics are unwilling to relinquish their respective habits. For them, the positive effects override harmful consequences.

However with progression, problems continuously amass, and these add a new dimension to gambling or to drinking. The pathological gambler no longer gambles solely for excitement, distraction, or monetary rewards; he or she gambles to eliminate distress. The need for escape rapidly overshadows other reasons for gambling. The same process occurs for alcoholics and their drinking. Faced with problems, but not wanting to relinquish their habits, pathological gamblers and alcoholics try moderation. Many are not successful. Because moderation doesn't work for these individuals, and because they believe that abstinence is not a viable alternative, they cling to their disorders. This being the case, it is interesting that many individuals do give up their drinking or gambling.

Why Do Some People Stop Drinking or Gambling

Even though pathological gamblers and alcoholics appear committed to their respective habits, for some, a significant event like losing one's job, a marriage breakdown, a hospitalization, or an arrest, makes them realize that they have a problem. In cases like this, some people are able to walk away from their gambling or their drinking and never look back. Others have several relapses before they commit to abstinence. Some voluntarily enter a treatment program. However, there are many cases in which, despite problems, individuals resist giving up their gambling or their drinking. In situations like this, intervention often is necessary.

Intervention

An intervention is an attempt to force the individual into treatment. It typically involves confronting the individual with the harmful consequences of his or her disorder, and stipulating the requirement of treatment. Because many people are in denial and resist intervention, consequences for noncompliance must be established. This is referred to as leverage. A crucial element of confrontation is that it be done in a firm, but caring and nonblaming manner.

Intervention is usually initiated by any person(s) who is close to the afflicted individual, including a spouse, friend(s), family member(s), employer, and so on. Sometimes the court system intervenes, ordering an individual to seek treatment. In other cases, a professional like a psychologist, physician, or member of the clergy, may intervene. For intervention to be effective, the relationship between the intervener(s) and the recipient must be one that is of value, and one which the pathological gambler or the alcoholic does not wish to put at risk. If the relationship between the intervener and the person in question is insignificant, the intervention will be ignored.

Intervention is both difficult and stressful, and may make matters worse if not properly performed. Consequently, an intervention must be well planned and not done on impulse.

Preparation for an Intervention

In my previous books (1989, 1992, 1995), I describe several reasons why individuals should carefully prepare for an intervention and seek professional consultation prior to doing so. First of all, consulting with a professional prior to an intervention allows the intervener(s) to vent his or her feelings, thus reducing the chance of blame during the intervention. Second, a professional consultation teaches the person(s) how to properly intervene, and how to therapeutically confront the individual. Third, a planned intervention helps the intervener to avoid enabling. A trademark of alcoholism and pathological gambling is the individual's ability to turn situations around and blame others. Professional consultation prepares the intervener for this. Fourth, professional consultation familiarizes the intervener with types of treatment services which are available, and how the entry processes works. Fifth, consulting with a professional also allows the potential intervener to carefully develop and evaluate the consequences, should the intervention be rejected. In the absence of viable consequences, interventions are rarely effective. The intervener must also be prepared to follow through with the consequences, should the intervention fail. To not do so enables the recipient to strengthen the disorder. Consequently, the intervener must establish consequences that are realistic and viable.

Problems with Intervention

While many interventions are successful and the person enters treatment, others do not go according to plan. In other words, the recipient of the intervention may be willing to risk the consequences, and, therefore, reject the intervention. Some alcoholics and pathological gamblers are so entrenched in their disorders, that abstinence is completely foreign to them. They go to great lengths to maintain their habits, including losing a job, marriage, family, and friends.

16
Treatment

Alcoholism

Recognizing the harmful consequences of their alcohol consumption, some alcoholics stop drinking and never again touch alcohol. Unfortunately, for the majority of alcoholics, recovery is not so simple. Prior to achieving sobriety, many individuals relapse. In other words, after periods of abstinence, they resume heavy drinking. Others never recover. Often, they die prematurely, either from physical complications, suicide, or violence.

Some alcoholics give up, and drink until they die. Despite this, recovery is possible for all, although it is more difficult for some than for others. Abstinence is what makes recovery intimidating. Alcoholics are so dependent upon pleasurable feelings, as well as the stress-reducing effects created by drinking, that abstinence makes them feel vulnerable. Although feelings of vulnerability are not usually permanent, alcoholics find it difficult to endure even temporary discomfort. They are quick to disregard the harmful consequences of their alcohol consumption and quick to relapse. To help the alcoholic weather the stress of early recovery, treatment is often necessary.

Treatment for alcoholism consists of several stages. The first stage helps alcoholics accept that they have a problem with their drinking, and that sobriety is the most viable alternative. This involves therapeutically challenging the alcoholic's belief system that they can drink safely. The individual is helped to understand alcohol consumption for what it really is.

The second stage of treatment helps the individual deal with and resolve emotional issues. This includes the resolution of problems created by their alcohol consumption. Some have uncomfortable memories from the past. Unless individuals in recovery deal with their problems, and uncomfortable feelings and memories, drinking will remain attractive. Alcohol consumption loses its appeal only after the recovering alcoholics feel better about themselves.

The third stage of treatment consists of encouraging recovering individuals to make healthy changes in their lifestyles. If people leave treatment and resume lifestyles that are the same as when they were drinking, this ensures a relapse. Alcoholism is an all-encompassing disorder. It weaves itself into most aspects of a person's lifestyle. Consequently, mere abstinence is insufficient for meaningful recovery. A meaningful lifestyle that promotes sobriety is necessary.

Treatment Programs for Alcoholism

All major cities in Canada and the United States have treatment centers for alcoholism (and other drug addictions). In the United States, alcoholism is treated through private clinics, and in some cases, state or local hospitals. In Canada, most programs are funded by provincial and federal governments and are offered at no charge for Canadian citizens.

Individuals who enter a treatment center can expect to go through some type of intake process to determine which program is best suited. In many cases, the intake process functions as the first step in helping clients recognize that a problem with alcohol exists. Once intake is completed, clients are usually referred to either residential (inpatient) or nonresidential (outpatient) programs. Some programs cater specifically to adults, whereas others specialize in the treatment of youths. Some treatment programs are coed, and others separate male and female clients. Program duration varies between centers, and may last from a few weeks to several months. Clients in treatment are encouraged to move through the three stages of recovery described in this chapter. Once treatment is completed, most centers offer some type of aftercare. Early sobriety is very intimidating for most recovering alcoholics, and aftercare offers support and guidance.

Like many other disorders, alcoholism varies in severity from person to person. Typically, individuals in the early stage of their alcoholism do not require the intense treatment indicated for late-stage alcoholics. In most cases, nonresidential programs suffice. Middle- and late-stage alcoholics typically require more intensive treatment, which may require a residential program. Individuals in alcohol withdrawal usually require a residential setting, where they can be medically monitored and treated.

Problem Drinkers

Problem drinkers differ from alcoholics in that they are potentially able to moderate their alcohol consumption and learn to drink in a social manner. Consequently, problem drinkers usually benefit from nonresidential programs. If a person's alcohol consumption is such that a residential program is warranted, then alcoholism, as opposed to problem drinking, is usually present.

Pathological Gambling

With a few exceptions, the treatment of pathological gambling is not unlike that for alcoholics. Pathological gamblers must be helped to recognize and to accept that a gambling problem exists. Emotional issues that may have precipitated, and those that sustain pathological gambling must be addressed and resolved. The recovering individual also must be aided in altering his or her way of living, in order to support a gambling-free existence.

As with alcoholics, the pathological gambler's denial system must be therapeutically challenged. Pathological gamblers must learn to deal with and resolve problems and discomfort in healthy ways, as opposed to gambling. For those who enjoy excitement, healthy alternatives must be explored. Unlike alcoholics, many pathological gamblers do not require residential programming. In certain cases, where an addiction to alcohol and/or other drugs also exists, residential programming, including a detoxification unit, may be indicated.

Recovery Process

Recovery from alcoholism and pathological gambling is the opposite of the process of deterioration caused by either disorder. First, alcoholics stop their drinking, and pathological gamblers stop their gambling. Gradually, the recovering individual comes to understand the nature of his or her problems. Through a combination of support, education and treatment, the individual's self-concept gradually improves. Healthy relationships are slowly established, and, along with proper nutrition and rest, the recovering person slowly develops hope. Family involvement in the treatment process aids family members in understanding what the recovering individual is experiencing and also helps family members resolve their feelings. Eventually, the recovering person's pattern of thinking and emotional control normalizes, and healthy relationships are established.

Prochaska, Norcross, and Diclemente (1994) describe how individuals often go through predictable stages of change. Although these stages apply generally, they are applicable to alcoholics and pathological gamblers. According to Prochaska et al., the first step in change is referred to as the Precontemplation Stage. Usually, people at this stage have no desire to change their behavior. They deny that a problem exists. Alcoholics and pathological gamblers active in their disorders, and in strong denial, are at this stage. Some people at this stage feel that the situation is hopeless, and this certainly applies to alcoholism and pathological gambling. Individuals in this stage usually attend treatment because of pressure from others, i.e., an intervention of some sort. With proper support and challenge, people enter the second stage, referred to as the Contemplation Stage. Here, the individual acknowledges that a problem exists, may even develop a solution, but is not yet ready to take action. Again, with proper support and challenge, the person moves to the Preparation Stage. Change is recognized as imminent, and plans are developed. The Action Stage follows and involves the overt modification of the person's behavior. During this stage, the individual is most vulnerable and, in the case of alcoholism and pathological gambling, requires extensive support and encouragement. The Maintenance Stage in which the individual attempts to consolidate his or her gains, and attempts to prevent relapse follows the Action Stage. The last stage, the Termination Stage, is where change is stabilized. The goal of alcoholism and pathological gambling treatment programs is to facilitate the individual's progress through these stages of change.

Self-Help Groups

Alcoholics Anonymous and Gamblers Anonymous offer self-help group support for individuals in recovery. The programs of AA and GA are based on the 12 steps of recovery, which indirectly incorporate the stages of change, described above. There are several advantages for the recovering alcoholic to attend AA and for the recovering pathological gambler to attend GA. One is the exposure of individuals new to recovery, to people who are experienced in recovery. Newcomers often receive beneficial advice and guidance from those who are experienced. A second advantage is that AA and GA act as counterbalances, to pressure for relapse. AA and GA also provide the advantage of a safe forum in which recovering individuals can share and explore their feelings, without fear of ridicule or misunderstanding. Experienced members provide advice and challenge denial in newcomers, thus helping to prevent relapses. Another advantage is that newcomers are exposed to healthy modeling influences, from those who are successful in recovery.

17
Other Drugs

Many alcoholics do not restrict their intoxicant consumption to alcohol. Some use other mood-altering drugs. In the same manner, many pathological gamblers either drink heavily and/or abuse other drugs. This chapter focuses upon the commonly abused mood-altering drugs.

Amphetamines

Amphetamines, and drugs related to amphetamines, stimulate the central nervous system. In other words, these drugs speed up the functioning of the body. Common amphetamines are Benzedrine, Dexedrine, Methedrine, and Ritalin. The street name for amphetamines is "uppers" or "speed."

Individuals use amphetamines for a variety of illicit reasons, including avoiding sleep so that one can drive or study for longer periods, attempting to improve athletic performance, and for the euphoric effects.

At low doses, the physical effects of amphetamines include decreased appetite, increased respiration, heart rate and blood pressure, and dilation of the pupils. Larger doses often result in a dry mouth, fever, diaphoresis, blurred vision, and dizziness. Extremely high doses produce a very rapid and irregular heart beat, tremors, loss of coordination, and possibly death caused by stroke or heart failure.

The psychological effects of low doses of these drugs include increased energy and alertness, a decrease in fatigue, and a sense of well-being. Greater doses result in restlessness, excitability, loquaciousness, and a sense of power. Higher doses may result in bizarre and repetitive behavior, aggressiveness, and hostility.

The long-term effects of using amphetamines include malnutrition and illness secondary to undereating. Typically, individuals who abuse these drugs are tired, irritable, depressed, and they sleep poorly. Some heavy users experience an amphetamine psychosis, which is a mental condition characterized by severe paranoia, agitation, and hallucinations. To lessen the uncomfortable side-effects of amphetamines and to maintain the euphoria, many chronic users rely upon other drugs, such as barbiturates, minor tranquilizers, alcohol, and opiates. This practice usually results in multiple drug dependence.

Amphetamines are physically addicting, and regular users develop tolerance and require increased doses to produce the same effects of lesser amounts. When chronic users stop using amphetamines, they commonly experience a detoxification syndrome, which includes disturbed and fitful sleep, excessive hunger, depression, and irritability. Sometimes, an individual may become suicidal. Also, abuse of amphetamines almost always results in significant psychological dependence, in which the person feels that he or she cannot exist without the drug.

Cocaine

Cocaine stimulates the central and sympathetic nervous systems. The effects are similar to those produced by amphetamines. The difference between cocaine and amphetamines is, that the former is a local anesthetic, the latter is not.

Cocaine is generally sold on the street as a hydrochloride salt, which is usually diluted with similar looking substances, such as sugar, talcum powder, or with drugs, such as procaine or amphetamines.

The most common way of taking cocaine into the system is through inhalation (snorting the drug into the nose). However, cocaine may also be applied to the mucus lining of the mouth, vagina, or rectum. The drug may also be taken into the system by intravenous injection, or by vaporizing and smoking it. In low doses, cocaine produces a euphoric feeling, with a sensation of enhanced mental alertness and sensory awareness, and increased energy. While under the influence of the drug, the user feels neither hungry nor tired. Larger doses intensify the euphoric effect, but may also lead to bizarre and even violent behavior. Physical symptoms include an increase in blood pressure, an acceleration in heart rate, a rise in body temperature, dilation of the pupils, diaphoresis, and an increase in respiration. Like amphetamines, cocaine may result in a toxic reaction that includes agitation, anxiety, increased reflex reaction, tremors, muscle twitching, hallucinations, paranoia, and delirium. Some individuals may even experience convulsions. As well, a cocaine overdose may result in a high fever, heart failure, or stroke. Chronic use of cocaine results in malnutrition, irritability, depression, paranoia, and for individuals who inject the drug, the risk of infections, including AIDS.

Cocaine is both physically and psychologically addicting. Regular heavy use results in tolerance, and a withdrawal syndrome that includes fatigue, fitful sleep, excessive hunger, irritability, depression, and in some cases suicidal ideation. Individuals become very psychologically dependent upon the drug, and they experience strong psychological cravings during the first several months of abstinence.

LSD and Other Hallucinogens

Hallucinogens are a class of drugs that produce significant changes in an individual's mental state and mood. LSD, or Lysergic Acid Diethylamide, is the most popular hallucinogen.

LSD is usually taken orally, but the drug may also be inhaled or injected. Although the effects of all psychoactive or mood-altering drugs are influenced by mental set, attitude and expectations are most significant for hallucinogens. Consequently, the effect of LSD (and other hallucinogens) depends not only on the amount of the drug taken, but also on the experience and the mental and emotional state of the user. In other words, depending upon how the user feels when the drug is ingested, taking LSD may result in either a pleasant or unpleasant experience.

LSD produces a rapid increase in blood pressure, body temperature, and heart rate. Pupils are dilated, muscles are weak, and individuals may experience nausea, tremors, chills, a loss of appetite, and deep and rapid breathing. Very high doses of LSD may produce convulsions.

Typically, while under the influence of LSD, the individual experiences aberrations in thinking, feeling, and perception, including competing emotions, labile mood, and significant stimulus distortion. As well, the individual's sense of time is disturbed, and the user has difficulty differentiating the boundaries of self and objects. For some people, the LSD experience may be very pleasant, and for others it may be threatening and result in panic.

Long-term effects of LSD include flashbacks, which are spontaneous and unpredictable recurrences of an LSD experience. Flashbacks may occur even after months or more of abstinence from LSD. Chronic use of LSD also results in depression and anxiety.

Tolerance to LSD develops rapidly, such that after several days of continuous use, the individual no longer experiences the drug's effect. However, tolerance also diminishes rapidly, and is lost after a few days of abstinence. Consequently, LSD is usually taken on an irregular basis, thus allowing tolerance to diminish and the drug to regain its psychoactive effect.

Chronic users of LSD may develop psychological dependence. However, there is no evidence that regular use results in physical dependence. Although tolerance develops rapidly with continuous use, usually there is no significant and consistent detoxification reaction following abstinence.

Besides LSD, there is a variety of other hallucinogens. Commonly used ones are mescaline and psilocybin. The former is extracted from the peyote cactus, and the latter from particular types of mushrooms.

Minor Tranquilizers

Minor tranquilizers, otherwise known as sedatives or anxiolytics (anti-anxiety agents) are used therapeutically for the treatment of anxiety and insomnia. Low doses of these drugs usually produce feelings of relaxation and a sense of well-being. However, in a few cases, these drugs have been known to result in a loss of inhibition, or to cause dizziness, lethargy, and nausea. Besides being used in the treatment of anxiety and insomnia, other common therapeutic uses of minor tranquilizers include the treatment of certain seizure disorders, and muscle spasms.

Consistent use of sedatives may result in tolerance to the anxiolytic effect, causing some people to increase the dose. As a consequence, chronic use of sedatives may result in both psychological and physical dependence.

The withdrawal syndrome from sedatives, especially after long-term use, varies in intensity from insomnia, anxiety, restlessness, and irritability, to possible convulsive seizures and delirium. Withdrawal symptoms also may include excessive perspiring, tremors, and muscle weakness.

Although most individuals who use sedatives, do so through medical prescription, there are some who purchase sedatives from the street. Many use sedatives for the reverie that large doses produce, and others rely on sedatives to combat the aversive effects of cocaine and amphetamines.

Barbiturates

Barbiturates are sedatives closely related to minor tranquilizers. Common barbiturates include amobarbital, phenobarbital, and secobarbital.

Small doses of barbiturates produce feelings of calmness and muscle relaxation, and relieve anxiety and depression. For some people, higher doses often result in sleep, whereas for others, high doses result in feelings and behaviors similar to alcohol intoxication, including a "high" feeling, slurred speech, ataxic gait, and impaired reaction time. Very high doses may result in respiratory and cardiac arrest.

Individuals may become both psychologically and physically dependent upon barbiturates. Using barbiturates for their euphoric mood-altering effects often results in abuse, leading to physical dependence including high tolerance, and a withdrawal syndrome that may be life-threatening. Detoxification includes restlessness, anxiety, insomnia, and possible delirium and convulsive seizures. Psychological dependence is reflected in a powerful emotional need to continue using the drug.

Opiates

Opiates are extracted from the juice of the Asian poppy. Opiates include opium, codeine, morphine, and heroin. Opiates are used therapeutically for the relief of pain resulting from disease, injury, or surgery. Depending on the type of opiate, the drug may be ingested orally, smoked, or taken into the system by intravenous injection.

Ingestion of opiates produce a sense of pleasure that overrides feelings of hunger, pain, thirst, and sexual desire. The body feels warm, and the mouth feels dry. High doses, especially when the drug is injected or smoked, results in a surge of ecstasy, followed by state of pleasant drowsiness. Overdoses may result in respiratory depression and cardiac arrest.

Chronic use of opiates may result in both psychological and physical dependence. Individuals become psychologically oriented toward having the drug, and physically, tolerance develops and withdrawal symptoms are significant. The symptoms include yawning, fatigue, crying, nausea, diarrhea, abdominal cramping, runny nose, irritability, tremors, and the chills.

Cannabis

Marijuana consists of the tops, dried leaves, seeds, and bits of the stem of the *cannabis sativa* plant. Hashish is the dried resin that comes from the flowers and leaves of the female plant. Hash oil is the oily extract of the *cannabis* plant. Hashish and hash oil are higher in concentration of THC (the psychoactive component) than marijuana.

Marijuana is typically smoked in cigarettes, referred to as joints. Hashish is often mixed with tobacco and smoked. Hash oil is typically put on the end of a tobacco or marijuana cigarette and smoked. Marijuana, hashish, and hash oil may also be mixed with certain food preparations and cooked. However the psychoactive effect is less intense, than if the drug is smoked.

The short-term effects of any cannabis substance include a feeling of euphoria, in which the individual tends to talk and laugh more than usual. Typically, the person experiences an increased heart rate, a reddening of the eyes, and occasional fatigue. Larger doses may result in a distortion in perception of stimuli. Use of *cannabis* products results in an impairment of short-term memory, attention, logical thinking, and physical coordination. High doses may create effects similar to hallucinogens.

Heavy *cannabis* users, like heavy cigarette smokers, may develop chronic bronchitis and other respiratory diseases. Chronic users also show a loss of motivation and energy, confused thinking, and apathy. Because THC is fat soluble, chronic use results in a buildup of the psychoactive substance in the body. With chronic use, both physical tolerance and psychological dependence may occur.

Inhalants

Inhalants include solvents, plastic cement, model airplane glue, various thinners, nail-polish remover, gasoline, and so on. Inhaling the vapors from these particular chemicals results in feelings of euphoria, dizziness, vivid fantasies, and excitement. Individuals also experience nausea, poor muscle coordination, depressed reflexes, light sensitivity, and they sneeze and cough a lot. While under the influence of inhalants, the person may become disoriented, hallucinate, lose consciousness, and experience convulsive seizures.

Physically chronic inhalant users experience fatigue, thirst, weight loss, nose bleeds, red eyes, sores about the nose and mouth, and a pallor. Long-term use may also result in liver and kidney damage. Psychologically, long-term users of inhalants demonstrate irrational thought, depressed affect, irritability, feelings of persecution, and hostility. In some cases, users may develop Organic Brain Syndrome (brain damage), characterized by poor motor coordination and impaired mental functioning.

Inhalant use may result in physical and psychological dependence. Tolerance develops whereby increasingly greater doses are required to produce the euphoric effect, and withdrawal symptoms may include abdominal pains, headaches, muscle cramps, hallucinations, and delirium.

Bibliography

Ainslie, G. "Behavioral Economics II: Motivated Involuntary Behavior," *Social Science Information* 23 (1984): 735-79.

American Psychiatric Association. *Diagnostic and Statistical Manual of Mental Disorders,* Third Edition, Washington, D.C., 1980.

American Psychiatric Association. *Diagnostic and Statistical Manual of Mental Disorders,* Third Edition Revised, Washington, D.C., 1987.

American Psychiatric Association. *Diagnostic and Statistical Manual of Mental Disorders,* Fourth Edition, Washington, D.C., 1994.

Anderson, G., and R. Brown. "Real and Laboratory Gambling, Sensation Seeking, and Arousal," *British Journal of Psychology* 75 (1984): 401-10.

Bandura, A. *Principles of Behavior Modification.* New York: Holt, Rinehart, and Winston, 1969.

Bergh, C., and E. Kuhlhorn. "The Development of Pathological Gambling in Sweden." *Journal of Gambling Studies* 10/3 (1994): 261-74.

Blaszczynski, A., W. Simon, and N. McConaghy. *Plasma Endorphin Levels in Pathological Gambling.* Paper presented at the Sixth International Conference on Gambling and Risk Taking, Atlantic City, 1984.

Braucht, G. N. "Problem Drinking Among Adolescents: A Review and Analysis of Psychosocial Research," *Alcohol and Health Monograph* 4 U.S. Department of Health and Human Services (1982): 143-64.

Brenner, B. "Alcoholism and Fatal Accidents," *Quartery Journal of Studies on Alcohol,* 28/3 (1967): 517-28.

Brown, R. "Classical and Operant Paradigms in the Management of Compulsive Gamblers," *Behavioural Psychotherapy* 15 (1987): 111-22.

Brown, R. "Pathological Gambling and Associated Patterns of Crime: Comparisons with Alcohol and other Drug Addictions," *Journal of Gambling Behavior* 3 (1987): 98-114.

Bruce, A. C., and J. E. V. Johnson. "Male and Female Betting Behaviour: New Perspectives," *Journal of Gambling Studies* 2 (1994): 183-98.

Carlton, P., and P. Manowitz. "Behavioral Restraint and Symptoms of Attention Deficit Disorder Disorder in Alcoholics and Pathological Gamblers." *Neuropsychobiology* 25 (1992): 44-48.

Christiansen, B. A., and S. A. Brown. *Adolescent Alcohol Expectance: Further Evidence of their Robust Nature.* Paper presented at the annual meeting of the American Psychological Association, Los Angeles, 1985.

Ciarrocchi, J. W. "Rates of Pathological Gambling in Publicly Funded Outpatient Substance Abuse Treatment." *Journal of Gambling Studies* 9/3 (1993): 289-93.

Ciarrocchi, J., and A. Hohmann. "The Family Environment of Married Male Pathological Gamblers, Alcoholics, and Dually-Addicted Gamblers." *The Journal of Gambling Behavior* 5 (4) (1989): 283-91.

"Core Knowledge in the Drug Field," *Non-Medical Use of Drugs Directorate,* National Health and Welfare, Ottawa, Ontario, 1978.

Core Knowledge: Substance Abuse Field, Drug Use and Abuse; Then and Now. Winnipeg, Manitoba: Addictions Foundation of Manitoba, 1978.

Culleton, R. P. *A Survey of Pathological Gamblers in the State of Ohio.* Philadelphia: Transition Planning Associates, 1985.

Cummings, C., J. Gordon, and G. Marlatt. "Relapse: Strategies of Prevention and Prediction," in W. R. Miller (ed.), *The Addictive Behaviors.* Oxford: Pergammon, 1980.

Custer, R., and H. Milt. "When Luck Runs Out," *Facts on File Publication,* New York: 1985.

Dackis, C. A., and M. S. Gold, M.S. "New Concepts in Cocaine Addiction, The Dopamine Depletion Hypothesis," *Neuroscience and Behavioral Reviews* 9 (1985): 469-77.

Dickerson, M. G. "Gambling: Dependence Without a Drug," *Int. Rev. Psychiatry* 1 (1989): 157-72.

Epstein, J. "Confessions of a Low Roller." In R. Atwan (ed.), *The Best American Essays,* New York: Ticknor and Fields, 1989.

Fell, J.C. *Alcohol Involvement in Traffic Accidents: Recent Estimates from the National Center for Statistics and Analyses,* NHTSA Technical Report No. DOT HS-806 269, Washington, D.C.: National Highway Traffic Safety Administration, p. 27, 1982.

Fifth Special Report to the U.S. Congress on Alcohol and Health, Secretary of Health and Human Services, U.S. Department of Health and Human Services (1983): 83-99.

Fishman, R. *The Encyclopedia of Psychoactive Drugs: Alcohol and Alcoholism.* New York: Chelsea House Publishers, 1992.

Freedman, J. L. *Introductory Psychology.* Don Mills, Ontario: Addison-Wesley Publishing, 1978.

Glen, A. M. *Personality Research on Pathological Gamblers.* Paper presented at the American Psychological Association Annual Convention, New York, August 1979.

Griffiths, M. "Tolerance in Gambling: An Objective Measure Using the Psychophysiological Analysis of Male Fruit-Machine Gamblers." *Addictive Behaviors* 18 (1993): 365-72.

Griffiths, M. "The Acquisition, Development and Maintenance of Fruit-Machine Gambling in Adolescence." *Journal of Gambling Studies* 6 (1990): 193-204.

Henry, S. L., "Pathological Gambling: Etiologic Considerations and Treatment Efficacy of Eye Movement Desensitization/Reprocessing." *Journal of Gambling Studies* 12/4 (1996): 395-405.

Herridge, P., and Gold, M. S. "Pharmacological Adjuncts in the Treatment of Opiod and Cocaine Addicts." *Journal of Psychoactive Drugs* 20/3 (July/September 1988): 233-42.

Herscovitch, A. *Cocaine: the Drug and the Addiction.* Lake Worth, Fla.: Gardner Press, 1996.

Herscovitch, A. "Drug Dependence: From Recognition to Recovery," *Addiction Research Foundation,* Toronto, Ontario: 1992.

Herscovitch, A. *Alcoholism: From Recognition to Recovery.* Toronto, Ontario: Addiction Research Foundation, 1989.

Hyman, S. E. "Why Does the Brain Prefer Opium to Broccoli?" *Harvard Review of Psychiatry* 2 (1994): 43-46.

Hyman, S. E., and E. J. Nestler. *The Molecular Foundations of Psychiatry.* Washington, D.C.: American Psychiatric Press, 1993.

Jacobs, D. F. "A General Theory of Addictions: Rationale for and Evidence Supporting a New Approach for Understanding and Treating Addictive Behaviors." In H. J. Shaffer, S.A. Stein, D. Gambino, and T. N. Cummings (eds.), *Compulsive Gambling: Theory, Research, and Practice.* Lexington, B.C.: Heath and Company, 1989, p. 35-64.

Jacobs, D. F. "Behavioral Aspects of Gambling: Evidence for a Common Dissociative-like Reaction Among Addicts," *Journal of Gambling Behavior* 4 (1988): 27-37.

Jacobs, D. F., C. Elia, and M. Goldstein et al. *Prevalence of Problem Gambling among Hospitalized Male Adult Substance Abusers.* Paper presented at the Fifth National Conference on Gambling Behavior, Duluth, Minn., July 1991.

Jaffe, A., and C. Lohse. "Expectations Regarding Cocaine Use: Implications for Prevention and Treatment." *Addictions and Recovery* (May/June 1991): 9-12.

Kissin, B. "Theory and Practice in the Treatment of Alcoholism." In *Treatment and Rehabilitation of the*

Chronic Alcoholic, B. Kissin and H. Begleiter (eds.), New York: Plenum Press, 1977.

Ladouceur, R., and C. Mireault. "Gambling Behaviors among High School Students in the Quebec Area." *Journal of Gambling Behavior* 4 (1988): 3-12.

Landry, M., and D. Smith. "Crack: Anatomy of an Addiction." *California Nursing Review* 9/2 (March/April 1987): 8-47.

Langer, E.J. "The Illusion of Control." *Journal of Personality and Social Psychology,* 32 (1975): 311-28.

Lee, A. *A Synopsis of Anaesthesia,* Fourth Edition. Bristol: John Wright and Sons Ltd., 1959.

Legg England, S., and K. G. Gotestam. "The Nature and Treatment of Excessive Gambling." *Acta Psychiatr. Scand.* 84 (1991): 113-20.

Lesieur, H. R. "The Female Pathological Gambler." In Eadington, W.R. ed. *Gambling Studies: Proceedings of the Seventh International Conference on Gambling and Risk Taking,* Reno, Nev.: University of Nevada, 1988.

Lesieur, H. R. *The Chase: Career of the Compulsive Gambler.* Cambridge, Mass.: Schenkman, 1984.

Lesieur, H. R., and S. B. Blume. "When Lady Luck Loses: Women and Compulsive Gambling," *Feminist Perspectives on Addictions,* N. Van Den Bergh (ed.), New York: Springer Publishing Company, 1991, p. 181-97.

Lesieur, H. R., and S. B. Blume. "The South Oaks Gambling Screen (the SOGS); A New Instrument for the Identification of Pathological Gamblers." *American Journal of Psychiatry* 144 (1987): 1184-88.

Lesieur, H. R., S. B. Blume, and R. M. Zoppa. "Alcoholism, Drug Abuse, and Gambling." *Alcoholism: Clinical and Experimental Research* 10 (1986): 33-38.

Livingston, J. *Compulsive Gamblers: Observations on Actions and Abstinence.* New York: Harper Torchbooks, 1974.

Lorenz, V. *Differences Found Among Catholic, Protestant and Jewish Families of Pathological Gamblers.* Paper presented at the Fifth National Conference on Gambling and Risk Taking, Lake Tahoe, Nev., October 1981.

Lorenz, V.. and D. E. Shuttlesworth. "The Impact of Pathological Gambling on the Spouse of the Gambler." *Journal of Community Psychology* 11 (1983): 67-76.

Lorenz, V. C., and R. A. Yaffe. "Pathological Gambling: Psychosomatic, Emotional, and Marital Difficulties as Reported by the Gambler," *Journal of Gambling Behavior* 2 (1986): 40-49.

Milkman, H. B., and S. G. Sunderwith. *Craving for Ecstacy: The Consciousness and Chemistry of Escape.* Lexington, Mass.: Lexington Books, 1987.

Miller, W. "Individual Outpatient Treatment of Pathological Gambling," *Journal of Gambling Behavior* 2/2 (1986): 95-107.

National Institute on Alcohol Abuse and Alcoholism. *Alcohol and Health Monograph 3: Prevention, Intervention and Treatment.* Rockville, Md.: 1982, 136-37.

Nesse, R. M., and K. C. Berridge. "Psychoactive Drug Use in Evolutionary Perspective," *Science* 278 (1977): 63-66.

Prochaska, J. O., J. C. Norcross, and C. C. Diclemente. *Changing for Good.* New York: Avon Books, 1994.

Ramirez, L. F., R. A. McCormick, A. M. Russo et al. "Patterns of Substance Abuse in Pathological Gamblers Undergoing Treatment," *Addictive Behavior* 8 (1984): 425-28.

Reid, R.L. "The Psychology of the Near Miss," *Journal of Gambling Behavior* 2 (1986): 32-39.

Rosenthal, R. J. "Pathological Gambling," *Psychiatric Annals* 222 (February 1992):72-78.

Roy, A., B. Adinoff, L. Roehrich, R. Custer, V. Lorenz, and M. Linnoila. *A Search for Biological Substrates to Pathological Gambling.* Paper presented at the Seventh International Conference on Gambling and Risk Taking, Reno: University of Nevada-Reno, 1988.

Ruch, F. L., and P. G. Zimbardo. *Psychology and Life,* Eighth Edition. London, England: Scott, Foresman, and Company, 1971.

Rugle, L. J. "Initial Thoughts on Viewing Pathological Gambling from a Physiological and Intrapsychic Structure Perspective," *Journal of Gambling Studies,* 9 (1) (1993): 3-15.

Schmidt, W., and J. de Lint. "Cause of Death of Alcoholics," *Quarterly Journal of Studies on Alcohol* 33/1 (1972): 171-85.

Shaffer, H. J. "Understanding the Means and Objects of Addiction: Technology, the Internet, and Gambling," *Journal of Gambling Studies* 12/4 (1996); 461-69.

Shaffer, H. J., M. N. Hall, J. S. Walsh, and J. Vander Bilt. "The Psychosocial Consequences of Gambling." In R. Tannenwald (ed.), *Casino Development: How Would Casinos Affect New England's Economy.* Special Report

No. 2. Boston: Federal Reserve Bank of Boston, 130-141, 1995.

Shain, M. "Alcohol, Drugs and Safety: An Updated Perspective on Problems and their Management in the Workplace." *Acccident Analysis and Prevention* 14/3 (1982): 239-46.

Shulman, G. "Alcoholism and Cocaine Addiction: Similarities, Differences, Treatment Implications," *Alcoholism Treatment Quarterly* 4/3 (1987): 31-40.

Smith, D. "Decreasing Drug Hunger," *Professional Counselor* (November/December 1986): 6.

Specker, S. M., G. A. Carlson, K. M. Edmonson, P. E. Johnson, and M. Marcotte. "Psychopathology in Pathological Gamblers Seeking Treatment," *Journal of Gambling Studies* 12/1 (1996): 67-81.

The National Information Center on Legalized and Compulsive Gambling. *Teenage Gambling in America,* 1/1 (July 1991) cited in the training manual (Phase II) of the Minnesota Council on Compulsive Gambling, (1993): 117.

Volberg, R. A. *Estimating the Prevalence of Pathological Gambling in the United States.* Presented at the Eighth International Conference on Risk and Gambling, London, England, 1990.

Volberg, R. A., and H. J. Steadman. "Prevalence Estimates of Pathological Gambling in New Jersey and Maryland." *American Journal of Psychiatry* 146 (1989): 1618-19.

Volberg, R. A., and H. J. Steadman. "Refining Prevalence Estimates of Pathological Gambling." *American Journal of Psychiatry* 145 (1988): 502-5.

Walters, G. "The Gambling Lifestyle: I. Theory," *Journal of Gambling Studies* 10/2 (1994): 159-82.

Wexler, S. *A Chart on the Effects of Compulsive Gambling on the Wife.* Parlin, N.J.: 1981.

Wickelgren, I. "Getting the Brain's Attention," *Science,* 278 (1997): 35-37.

Wikler, A. "Recent Progress in Research on the Neuro-physiological Basis of Morphine Addiction," *American Journal of Psychiatry* 105 (1948): 328-38.

Wray, I., and M. Dickerson. "Cessation of High Frequency Gambling and 'Withdrawal' Symptoms," *British Journal of Addiction* 76 (1981): 401-05.